A Bulletproof Life
A Street Cop's Answer to All of Life's Threats

G.T. Gentry

A Bulletproof Life
A Street Cop's Answer to All of Life's Threats
by G.T. Gentry

Printed in the United States of America

ISBN 978-1-60647-816-5

Edited by R.R. Hart

Author's Note
Names and dates may have been altered to protect the identities of those who wish to remain anonymous. Additionally, the stories herein are based on the author's actual experiences for the purpose

of illustration. They do not necessarily represent all of the facts and/or details and may include certain fictional representation. All cases however, are considered "Closed" as they relate criminally, civilly and departmentally.

www.xulonpress.com

Endorsements for *Bulletproof*...

"Finally, someone has written a book that I would feel comfortable recommending to my buddies regardless of where they are on their spiritual journey with God. Jesus was the master story teller in his ability to connect unknown spiritual truth with familiar, everyday scenarios. Gentry has taken those same Biblical truths and connected them with the raw, gritty reality of the streets of a crime filled city in parable style teaching. Like watching an action film or a TV cop show, *A Bulletproof Life* is a, "must read"... an, "I couldn't put it down." I believe that *A Bulletproof Life* could be the "bullet" that God uses to pierce the defensive "Kevlar" that surrounds our hearts."
-Jim Burgen, Pastor, Flatirons Community Church, Lafayette CO

"Todd Gentry is a fearless, devoted police officer who is the terror of criminals and the hero of citizens who live in fear of predators. This book is a piercing look into the [cop] soul and for those [cops] who are worn down by the bullets of ambiguity, heartbreaking tragedy and cynicism; it is the vest that will save their health and their soul."
–Mike O'Neill, Police Commander (ret.)

"*A Bulletproof Life* is an absorbing book about life. Although written by a police officer chronicling his experience in the dangerous world of law enforcement in a major city, it should resonate with civilians and police officers alike in it's applicability toward handling the challenges that life throws at us.

Officer Gentry is a true "Sheepdog" in the classic sense as we have come to know that term based on the work of Lt. Col. David Grossman. As a former Marine, I appreciate how it is said that Marines "move toward the sound of the guns." Like a good Marine, Officer Gentry is one of those cops who moves toward the sound of the gun and does not flinch. He takes his role as Sheepdog seriously which becomes obvious from the stories that he shares with the reader.

What truly sets this book apart from others is the way Todd interweaves the spiritual with the everyday challenges of a street cop. He gives a new meaning to the word "bulletproof" that should serve as a lesson and an inspiration to all of us. There is a lot in this book. I recommend that the book be read slowly and reflectively. Its lessons could change your life."

-Tim Hall, Former U.S. Marine (Vietnam)

"We live in a troubled world. The threats are real. I have had the privilege of spending untold hours in Police units and working with Law Enforcement officers in many parts of our great country. I have had many memorable "ride-a-longs" but none so memorable as the written ride-a-long with Todd Gentry. Join Todd as he shares terror, tactics and even some laugh out loud adventures. When it's all over you will have a new found appreciation for body armor and spiritual armor; for the visible world and the invisible world."

-Gino Geraci, Chaplain, Denver F.B.I.
Pastor, Calvary South Denver, Littleton, CO

For Shane

CONTENTS

FOREWORD

B ulletproof. No one is really "bulletproof"...right? We
don't even use that word much anymore, preferring to
use the more precise term of "body armor" instead of the old,
outdated term "bulletproof vest."

I teach cops and military. I'm on the road almost 300
days a year training our most elite warriors. I call my class,
"The Bulletproof Mind: Mental Prep for Combat." But
everyone knows I'm using the term "bulletproof" metaphori-
cally. Technically speaking, nothing and no one is ever *really*
"bulletproof." Right?

God is.

Well, yeah. But He's God! He can do anything. That's
what "omnipotent" means. But you're not God! You can't
be bulletproof...can you? You can if God makes you bulletproof. *That* is what "omnipotent" means.

Permit me to share my favorite Psalm with you. It is a
short little piece of ancient poetry that is often called, "The
Traveler's Psalm."

When I was going thru Ranger school, my Ranger buddy
and I claimed this Psalm for ourselves. We would be shud-
dering with cold and misery. We had gone days without food
or sleep. And as the Big-Heat-Tab-in-the-Sky cracked above
the horizon and began to flood our miserable little universe

with light and warmth, my Ranger buddy would whisper, "Read our Psalm, Dave."

So listen, my friend, for here are the Words. The most ancient and powerful of Words. Words to provide solace in times of trial.

Like all poetry, it should be read aloud. Or if you are in a public place you can whisper them quietly to yourself:

I will lift up mine eyes unto the hills,
from *whence* cometh my help?
My help cometh from the *Lord!*

Behold! *He* will not suffer thy foot to slip.
He that keepeth Israel
shall neither slumber nor sleep.

The *Lord* is thy keeper;
the Lord is thy *shade* upon thy right hand.
He shall not suffer the sun to smite thee by day,
nor the moon by night.

The Lord shall preserve thee from *all* evil!
[How?!]
He shall preserve thy *soul!*

The *Lord* shall preserve thy going out,
and thy coming in;
from this day forth,
and even *forever* more.

You see, the greatest miracle is not to preserve this mortal flesh; flesh that passes in the blink of an eye, as the flowers of the field do fade. God's greatest gift is to preserve and protect our immortal soul!

Permit me now to share with you one of my favorite historical examples. During the early days of World War II, the British Army was trapped on the coast of France in a place called Dunkirk. The situation was grim. They were outnumbered, overwhelmed and defeated, on a narrow strip of beach with their backs to the sea. Across the English Channel the British were desperately scrambling to prepare an evacuation fleet consisting of every scow and fishing boat available. "Hold out!" England told her troops. "We will rescue you!" The commander of the besieged British forces sent back a three word answer: "But if not..."

But. If. Not! These were the words of the three Hebrew children about to be thrown into the fiery furnace in the Book of Daniel. "Our God shall preserve us," they said. *"But if not,* He is *still* God." That British commander was bulletproof. He had faith, and he was communicating to a culture steeped in faith, who understood the deep meaning of a simple three-word message.

You think yourself cursed and forlorn? Have faith! However bad it is, our God will preserve us. He will show us the path home from any dark and lonely place. *But if not,* He is *still* God and He has promised to preserve our *souls!*

And, aye, verily, He did rescue the British army, trapped on that beach. It has been referred to as the Miracle of Dunkirk. Every fishing boat and rinky-dink civilian pleasure craft that could float came across the English Channel that night in perfect weather, the clouds kept the German aircraft away and the evacuation went flawlessly.

But even if He doesn't rescue our flesh and blood bodies, His greatest miracle is to preserve our sad, sorry souls. The Almighty *does* work miracles. He performs the greatest of all miracles, every day, by the countless thousands, as He saves the souls of those who have trusted in God.

You see, God does work miracles. He just does it in His own peculiar way, in His own sweet time. And God can make you bulletproof. He does it His way, not ours. So, wouldn't you like to live, *A Bulletproof Life?* Then read on, gentle reader. Read on and enjoy, because it is a heck of a ride, and learn. Learn the most important lesson of all.

Dave Grossman
Lt. Col. (ret.) USA
Author, *On Killing* and *On Combat*
www.killology.com

WARNING

What you are about to read is real. These are not stunts or scenes from your favorite TV cop shows or movies. The parties involved are professional police officers with extensive knowledge, training, experience and are equipped with proper safety equipment including; Kevlar level IIIA body armor, the Glock semiautomatic pistol, Oleoresin Capsicum otherwise known as pepper spray or mace, expandable batons or Billy clubs, Blackjacks or "saps", Peerless handcuffs, Motorola two-way radios and of course the 4.6L, V8, 250 hp, Ford Crown Victoria Police Interceptor. Do not attempt to recreate any of the situations depicted. The circumstances are fast and fluid with uncertain outcomes. Do not attempt to become a vigilante, break up bar brawls, contact, confront, chase or otherwise become involved in a physical altercation with a gang member, drug dealer, wife beater, rapist or any other suspect, as they may be armed with guns, knives or bombs and whatever you do, for the love of Pete, do not indulge in the consumption of excessive amounts of donuts, glazed or otherwise, without thorough training. Failure to adhere to this warning may lead to serious bodily injury and/or death.

1

FIRING SQUAD

*There is nothing more exhilarating than to be shot
at without result.*

-Winston Churchill

"**O**pen outer door!"
A tall, gangly man steps into the sally port. The
heavy steel door slams loudly behind him. He was wearing
his usual grey, wrinkled, cheap suit. Government issue.

"Open inner door!"

The yelling voices and slamming doors didn't faze him.
That's how he and every hack that worked for him entered
the prison and cell block D. Especially cell block D. One
door opens at a time. No one escapes.

"Warden on the block!"

The advisement wasn't for the inmates; it was for the
other guard's benefit. It meant, "Heads up, the boss is here."
The inmates could care less. For them it was just another day
in the joint.

The warden climbed the stairs to Tier 3 West and made
the walk down the cell block, passing the long row of bars.

As he passed each inmate's cell, a hand would poke through the bars, holding a mirror. That was the only way they could catch more than a glimpse of the person passing their cells. But the cons weren't interested so much as who was there or even what they were there for, just which convict was getting the news. Good or bad.

This was cell block D. A place of solitary confinement. A place where the worst of the worst lived in complete physical isolation. A place where the only human contact they had was when a guard would slide them a plastic food tray or escort them to the recreation cage one hour a day. It was a place of twenty-three hour lock down, seven days a week. Yes, this was cell block D. A place we called, "D-Block."* A place also known as Death Row.

Besides the minimal, physical interaction they had with other human beings, the cons in D-Block mostly just heard voices. Those voices were usually the eleven other men on the block, as they yelled from cell to cell, in an effort to keep their sanity. But the rest of the time, when the lights went out and the sound of the other men's voices subsided, the only voices they heard were the ones in their own head. Voices that would speak of nothing but regret and the number of days they had left.

It was never news that he wanted to give but at least he was man enough to give it personally. The warden stopped in front of cell number 12, Tier 3 West and dropped the bomb that inmate number 100492 had been waiting to hear for the past two and a half years.

"James, I'm sorry to tell you that the governor denied your request for clemency. Tomorrow morning at 9:00 a.m., you will be put to death by firing squad. I'm sorry."

There weren't any hard feelings. He was after all, found guilty and the sincerity in the warden's voice was genuine. It always was.

"Do you have a final request that we can carry out for you?"

There was a long pause. Sitting on his bunk, staring at the floor, the convict rubbed his jaw, obviously in deep thought.

The warden waited patiently, knowing that even a man who has had the last two and a half years to ponder the answer to that question deserved a moment to be sure about it. James turned his head and looked at the warden through the bars. His right eyebrow raised and a smirk began to grow across his face.

"Why yes, a bulletproof vest."

That was convicted murderer, James Rodger's response on his final request before the firing squad.** And it has to be the best last request, ever.

"What?" The firing squad? I was planning on having the filet mignon and baked potato with my lethal injection. But now that I'm facing the firing squad, I think I'll take a bulletproof vest instead, please."

When bullets are imminent, we naturally seek protection. But what if we didn't wait until the last minute of our lives, like James Rodgers? What if we lived our whole lives bulletproof?

Because there's no doubt that life has a way of unloading on us. Sometimes it seems like sniper fire. A huge event hits us out of nowhere. A serious accident, a doctor's bad news, a family member's death. We stagger back, gasping for breath, trying to figure out what just happened.

Other times, life goes fully automatic on us. Illness, divorce, bills or job loss all come flying our way. We get hit with so many things that we don't know which way to turn. Feeling shredded to pieces, we're left in the rubble, lying for dead.

Sometimes, life just hits us like BB's from the end of the neighborhood kid's ten-pump, air rifle. Our boss is on our case, our coworkers are driving us crazy, our kids won't listen and our dog keeps peeing in the house. We feel angry, bitter and hurt. And while they may sound more annoying than deadly, they have the ability to somehow develop, deep within us, something that is often just as harmful.

And then, even when we have seemingly avoided all of those bullets in life, we still have to face life's threats from the gun in our very own hand; doubt, fear, insecurity, pride, selfishness, envy, greed, hate. I don't know which bullet in life is worse but I do know that they can all tear our lives apart just as effectively.

But what if there was a way to live a bulletproof life? What would life look like? I'm guessing that you probably wouldn't start chasing down drug dealers, shoot it out with terrorists, or attempt to defuse a bomb even though you're not sure which wire to cut but still feeling like you can because…well…you're bulletproof.

But seriously, what might your life *really* look like if you were bulletproof? Would you push life just a little further, a little faster and a little harder? Would you start to think, feel and act more like a superhero and less like a mortal? Would your life start to read more like a comic book and less like The Wall Street Journal? Or would everyday life just be different? Would you finally have enough guts to ask the hot chick out, brave enough to drive to work like a race car driver, bold enough to tell your boss what you really think or maybe just different enough to simply pull your shoulders back and walk through life a little taller, a little more confident and a little less afraid? The answers to those questions may not be what you're expecting.

They might just be more.

---

* My first law enforcement position was as a correctional officer for the Department of Justice (DOJ), Federal Bureau

of Prisons (BOP). I did in fact work D-Block, but it was a Disciplinary housing unit and not Death Row. I have however toured a facility used to perform death by lethal injection.

 ** James Rodgers statement of wanting a bulletproof vest as a last request before facing the firing squad was true although the story surrounding it was pure fiction and based on some of my real life experiences working in the joint.

2

WILD SIDE

Hell is empty and all the devils are here.

-William Shakespeare

Summer 2003

It was surreal. The car seemed to move in slow motion as we made our way down Detroit Avenue. The neon lights blurred in my peripheral vision as I drove but I knew what everyone of them read; motel, tattoos, liquor, and girls, girls, girls. I had finally made it as a cop six years ago and it was proving to be everything that TV had promised me that it would be, and more. I just couldn't believe the heat trapped between my bulletproof vest and body would be so unbearable. I let my arm hang out the window just above the, "To protect and serve" that was scrawled across the door. The breeze felt good as we drove.

Jimmy and I had arrested a street level drug dealer named, "Cuba" for possession and had just spent the previous two hours doing paperwork. It wouldn't have normally taken us that long to complete a simple dope case but this one had gotten bloody. And when you make 'em bleed, it can only mean one thing. More paperwork. But this one wasn't our fault. When we went to arrest him, Cuba tried to destroy the evidence by swallowing it. And while we were able to recover it before he could do that, he nearly bit his own tongue off in his attempt. Now, he was at the hospital, the bloody bag of crack cocaine was in the Evidence Bureau and we were headed back to the station.

I asked Jimmy, "Did you play poker last night?"

His response was immediate, "Yeah, I took first place."

Jimmy and I had gone through the police academy together. From there, we went on to work the same district and eventually partnered up when we made the Street Crime Arrest Team, or S.C.A.T. That's where we spent the next seven years swooping down and crushing crime by investigating and arresting enough drug dealers, gang bangers and prostitutes to earn us the street name, Batman and Robin.

Jimmy's excitement couldn't last. "It was crazy. I hit a nut flush on the first hand and tripled up. Then I just kept hitting aces all night long."

"What'd you win with?"

"Pair of aces with a queen kicker."

Figures, I thought. *The same hand you beat me with.* I was still happy for him and asked him how much he won.

"Sixteen hundred."

"Sixteen hundred?" I wanted to make sure I heard him right. That was equal to ten shifts of off duty work. Jimmy didn't respond a second time. The smirk on his face told me everything; that he loved the game just as much as the money.

There were several reasons that led to our now infamous name but the fact that Jimmy had dark wavy hair and rode shotgun were defining factors. He's a pistol that one, a real pit bull. What made him such a great poker player, despite the fact that he wouldn't do surveillance on a house for more than six minutes, was that he could wait all night long for the right cards. What made him such a great cop was the fact that he wasn't afraid to go, "All in." There were bigger guys out there to back you up, but if things went sideways, Jimmy was the one you could count on, with your life.

We continued to drive back to the station. I could have taken one of several routes but I always loved to drive Detroit Avenue.

Sex, drugs and rock and roll. Heroin, speed, crack or weed. Whatever you wanted, you could find on Detroit Avenue. It's the only place in the city that I've seen both transvestites and nuns on the same street. Heck, in this place, for all I know they were transvestite nuns.* It was just that wild. Yes, Detroit Avenue was our wild side and it didn't slow down when the rest of the city turned off the lights and went to bed. No, that's when the action just got started.

As we continued to drive, I noticed several hookers walking the beat. They're not hard to spot. This ain't *Pretty Woman* and they ain't Julia Roberts. Most of them are filthy and the only reason they're out there is to pay for their drug habit. Then there were a few dope dealers hanging out in the shadows, ironically, right under the spires of the Catholic Church cathedral. They try to stay visible to the cash paying customer without being seen by the passing cop. *I saw you but I'm on my way home. Maybe tomorrow...*

The addicts march along like zombies, smacking their lips and "tweaking" as we call it, for their next hit. They may not be sure where they're going, they just hope that wherever they end up there's enough crack cocaine to go around. Just past the capitol, we pass by a concert hall where thousands of kids wait in line. Their clothes are all black and their hair is spiked in every direction. As we pass by, they watch us with their eyes as their hands pass cigarettes back and forth. Their faces are painted black and white. Not like the old KISS fans. They're painted in a creepy clown sort of way. Without having to look at the marquee, I know it means that they're waiting to see the ICP, or Insane Clown Posse. And from the looks of them, they're as insane as the band's name suggests. I start to feel old.

We keep rolling. Another two miles of strip before we make our turn. It's still early but many of the homeless have already been drinking all day long. One pushes a shopping cart along with all of her life's belongings, another is urinating in the alley and the other is passed out on a bus bench. Then there are the, "Urban Pioneers." They're the same old Yuppies; they just moved from the Burbs to the hood. I guess that's the new "hip" thing to do. I watch as a few of them wade through this whole mess on their way to the newest and trendiest bar. Tomfoolery I say, tomfoolery!

I've never understood, even to this day, why anyone in their right mind would hang out here when the darkness settled in. The homeless were harmless. Don't bother them and they won't bother you. The wild side started when the addicts, prostitutes, dope dealers, gang bangers and freaks started fighting, robbing, stabbing, shooting and raping. And it doesn't matter if you're the suspect, victim, responding cop or innocent bystander just watching it all; if you're there, you're somehow a part of it, caught in the crosshairs of the wild side. It's as if you crossed an imaginary line of civilized society and the moment your foot hits the ground on the other side, you're in a jungle with no visible exit. But for the cops and robbers who choose to play, this is what's simply referred to as, "The Game."

The Game isn't played within the confines of a luxurious stadium, with freshly manicured grass and referees stopping play because of a foul. But don't let that fool you; the stakes are often just as high. The Game we play is played in the dark and dirty places of the inner-city. It's a game where the field is concrete and the ball that's fought over is often an eight-ball of crack, methamphetamine or heroin. It's a game where the other players don't play by the rules and where there are no timeouts. It's a game where winning or losing means life or death. This is The Game we play.

My mind absorbed all of this as I drove. At times, I've hated it. But most of the time, I can't get enough of it. The adrenaline, the arrests, the tricks good cops use and even the conflicts, fights and complaints are all part of it. Something about it is like a score for a junkie to me. Within my first year on the job, I had seen a mother and child who had been strangled to death, a man lying dead with the heroin needle still sticking out of his arm, a man shot nine times, another stabbed in the heart and several people mangled to death in car accidents. Then there were all the calls for service when we dealt with gang bangers, wife beaters, child abusers and lunatics. It was like driving by an accident scene. I didn't want to look away. I wanted to see all of the horror and ugliness and to save my piece of the world one crime at a time. Like it or not, I was addicted.

My mind drifted back six years earlier when I sat in the police academy on my last day there. With an almost proud gleam, like he was about to drop the best news we would ever hear, the police instructor said, "This job is your ticket to the greatest show on earth." And on Detroit Avenue, he was absolutely right.

Jimmy finally broke my wandering thought process.

"You working the bar tonight?"

While I was just a pauper, Jimmy was the overtime king. I really didn't feel like it. I was hot and tired and knew that we'd probably be fighting into the late hours of the night. I finally replied, "Yeah, I guess" with an enthusiasm in my voice that a pit bull, five years my younger, couldn't understand.

Blood Money

Take things as they are. Punch when you have to punch. Kick when you have to kick. -Bruce Lee

"You know that's blood money don't you?"

That's what the old cops or "Old Heads" called moonlighting at bars and nightclubs. They called it blood money because, well, someone often bleeds and sometimes that someone is you. I didn't understand their distaste for the whole idea. From their own war stories, you would have thought they lived for that. But I guess at some point, the thrill of fighting wears off and making a few extra bucks should be done as easy as possible. Jimmy and I hadn't reached that point yet. We hoped we never would.

Blood money? The whole job is blood money. We called it, Fight Club and Gladiator School. Blood money sounded too much like you did it because you had to. We went to Fight Club and Gladiator School because we wanted to and because it was a sure place to prove yourself when the opportunity came. And yes, sometimes someone bleeds and yes, sometimes that someone is us. But we're okay with that. The pure adrenaline it offered made it well worth it.

La Jeringa was my first fight club. In Spanish the name means, "The syringe." I suspect it got its name for the euphoric high that top shelf tequila shot through your veins like heroin did for the junkie. *La Jeringa* was a Mexican bar where Spanish rolled and liquor flowed. Don't use, "Mexican" in a derogatory way and don't insult them by being politically correct. These were Mexican Nationals and that pride ran deep. Last call meant buying beer by the bucket and a wrong word meant fists, boots and bottles were flying. It was dark, dirty and loud. Sure, *gringos* braved stepping in, just like the Urban Pioneers of Detroit Avenue, but if you drank too much and opened your mouth without thinking, there was a good chance that you'd wake up in the alley with a black eye, bloody nose and unsure what side of the border you were actually on.

It was a place where the *Mexican Federales* had long been forgotten. And that was unfortunate because a mere remembrance of them would have served us well. Just past midnight, every night, after the booze had been flowing hard and fast, order could turn into pure chaos, quick. Thus *La Policia* or, "The police." The two bouncers they employed weren't enough to keep things under control. If the bar wanted to continue making money hand over fist, they needed the cops and their authority there to do it. But these guys knew we had rules to play by, unlike every story of the *Federales* I'd ever heard and that fact seemed to be the catalyst that caused them to push our buttons on a nightly basis. So the safest way for us to maintain control was to send a message. A precedent of sorts.

"Welcome to *La Jeringa*. Have a good time. But if you're going to jack around, then be prepared to rumble because this is not *your* bar, it's *our* Fight Club."

That precedent didn't come easy. It never does.

0130 hours

It was a busy night. I knew that it would be. It almost always was. We had already thrown out at least twenty men that either wanted to fight or were too drunk to keep their heads off the bar top. Some went peacefully, others not so peacefully. It was just before last call when a fight erupted outside the bar. The pit bull stepped in to break it up but this time he didn't realize that he had just got in over his head. Which, by the way, is not an unusual occurrence for an, "All in" kind of guy.

As Jimmy tried to separate the two, I realized that this was the biggest Mexican man that I had ever seen. He didn't care too much for *La Policia* stepping in on his drunken adventure and took a swing at Jimmy. Before I could get there to help, another guy tried to jump in. With a flick of my wrist, my expandable baton was fully extended. I knew this was going to get ugly and that we had better finish it as fast as possible. I reared back and hit that guy as hard as I could. The sound of, "Whack!" emanated on contact like the sound of a whip. He went down and was completely out. I don't know if it was from the strike of my baton, the high consumption of alcohol, from crashing face first on the pavement or a combination of all three. But it really didn't matter at this point. The big guy still wanted to play.

And unfortunately, he had a brother. A big brother. And it was obvious that they weren't leaving that bar without proving they were willing to step into the gladiator ring. I wanted to get on my radio and ask for cover. This thing was well on its way out of control for two cops to handle. But even the short time it would have taken to do that would have left us exposed. It was now time for nothing else but to take care of business.

The two brothers refused our orders to leave and were not about to back down. They stood there defiant, fists balled up, ready to fight. Jimmy and I approached them. We hit each one with a blast of mace to the face, ordered them down to the ground, and when they refused, took them down with the ole' Billy club. And if you're wondering if the saying, "The bigger they are, the harder they fall" is true, both dropped like fresh cut Redwoods in the California forest.

Most of the bar had now filtered out into the parking lot and a crowd had developed. That's never a good thing. People began yelling and screaming in both English and Spanish and it was becoming potentially more dangerous. Despite three guys down, I had a feeling it wasn't quite over and unfortunately we had run out of handcuffs.

Then old Mr. Murphy reared his ugly head and whispered in my ear, "What can go wrong will go wrong."

Just then, another drunk wanted to fight and we were no longer in the playing mood. A well dressed *hombre* in a white button down shirt and white pants approached Jimmy. As he did, all I heard was Spanish, Spanish, *Mi famalia*, Spanish. The words, "my family" are all I understood. I assumed that he was related to one of the other three and didn't appreciate them being forcibly subdued to stop fighting. He took a full swing at Jimmy but Jimmy hit him first. The Mexican's face exploded like a *piñata* and he dropped like a rock. Bright red blood gushed from his nose and his entire white outfit was quickly soaked in his own blood. It was the single greatest punch that I've ever seen on the street.

That's enough Murph, let the rest of this turn out right...

As the fourth combatant laid there bleeding, it was obvious that he wasn't going anywhere. But with no handcuffs left, it was time to call for that cover. I slowed my breathing down, keyed my radio and calmly asked for a couple of cars Code 9 for a fight. Code nine meant a non-emergency response but apparently the subtle adrenaline in my voice, coupled with the fact we were working *La Jeringa,* sent a brigade of cops rolling in Code 10 with lights and sirens.

The sergeant arrived first and surveyed the scene. "God Almighty, what happened here?"

I gave him the obvious answer. "We had a bar fight."

With the huge crowd all around and four bodies strewn out across the parking lot, it looked like a battle scene from *Braveheart.*

"A bar fight?" he insisted.

"Yeah, a good ole' fashioned bar fight." I must have smirked because he wasn't appreciating my demeanor at this point and wanted the specifics.

"Long story short, Jimmy tried to break up a fight. That one right there tried to jump him and I hit him with my baton. Those two wanted to fight, refused to leave and were both maced and sticked. That one right there, in the white and red outfit, jumped in at the end and Jimmy busted his nose."

There was hours of paperwork coming and he didn't look happy. "All right, get an ambulance to check these guys and I'll meet you back at the station for a full report."

Two of the fighters were loaded into the ambulance and the other two were loaded into police cars. As we started back to the station, I was thankful that we came out of there without so much as a scratch but I was more proud of the fine display of fighting skills. Sure we used sticks and mace. But you come to our Fight Club without any toys to play with, that's your fault. Besides, there were four of them, two were huge and there is no such thing as a fair fight anyways. That's just the price you pay when you fight with the cops.

I know that one incident didn't make the precedent but it sure set the tone. As time went on, people still got drunk and got into fights but they never tried to mix it up with us like that again. Even more *gringos* began to show up. Months later, *La Jeringa* had calmed down enough that it became the setting where I was about to have one very interesting conversation...

That night I was working with Shane, another member of our team. As the evening wore on without any problems, we leaned back against the pool tables. From there, we could still watch most of the bar and started talking about work, life, politics and even religion. The smoke filled bar, loud Mariachi music and Spanish background noise seemed to make it a strange place for this conversation.

I asked Shane, "So how's life?"

"It's great. Everything's great. Work is great. My family is great." Then he paused, "Maybe too great. It makes me think something bad is going to happen."

That was Shane's proverbial, "What if" question.

Without saying it, his mind was wondering, "What if something happens to my life and I can't handle it? What if

I end up like the people on the street? What if my life turns out like the tragedies that I see everyday?"

I looked at this small but tough, bulletproof cop and sensed the fear in his mind. I had been there before myself. My worst nightmare wasn't about falling, being shot or having my weapon fail to operate the moment that I needed it the most. It was about the overlooked task of searching suspects and prisoners that I did hundreds of times a week and thousands of times a year. I dreamt that as I was searching a suspect, I reached into his pocket and was poked by a dirty heroin needle. As fast as I could reel back from the pain, I saw the skin on my hand become translucent and watched as the disease flowed through my veins, up my arm and across my chest. My skin began to boil like a pot of water on a hot stove and just as my flesh began to rot from my bones, I woke up in a cold sweat. It wasn't the fear of dying a long slow death that was so terrifying; it was the fear of living a life that I never imagined.

It was obvious, like my nightmare, that Shane was more afraid of what life may shoot at him than he was at taking a hit from a .45 caliber. He knew what that threat looked like and chose to face it everyday. But what about life? What do those threats look like? Debt. Foreclosure. Illness. Injury. Infidelity. Divorce. Death. We may have all been born into this world but we didn't sign up for a life like that. It makes us wonder such things as, "What if I can't pay the bills? What if we lose the house? What if I get cancer? What if I become disabled? What if my spouse leaves me? What if something happens to one of my kids?"

Those are all legitimate concerns and ones that we have no idea what the answer will be until they someday happen to us. And frankly, that scares us to death.

I didn't want to give Shane a stupid answer like, "Aw, don't worry. That'll never happen." I wasn't about to patronize a guy who had become a friend and who had legitimate fears. I was honest.

"Yeah, something bad might happen. Probably will, actually. They're just storms of life that hit us all sooner or later. That's just life. But what if you could be bulletproof from those things too?"

Bulletproof? From life? Man, is that possible?

Just as I could see the, "What if" wheels begin to turn in his head, the rest of our conversation was interrupted by the prick of a needle called *La Jeringa*. And it was time to fight. Again.

What if?

What if there was more to the wild side than just the murder, rape, child abuse, dead cops and tragic lives that the 80's rock band, Motley Crue sang about? What if there was more to the wild side than even all of the craziness that Detroit Avenue and *La Jeringa* dished out? What if the wild side is merely life itself? What if the wild side includes us and our own mistakes? What if the wild side looked a lot less like the dark side of life and looked a little more like…a morning commute?

Think about it. In the morning rush hour commute,

1) Every lane seems like a fast lane,
2) Everything that happens to the guy in front of you can happen to you, including, but not limited to: a cracked windshield, a blown tire, engine failure or an accident varying in severity from a minor fender bender to a bone crushing roll over and,
3) Nobody is doing everything right; everyone is breaking the law. From the intentional speeder to the *unintentional* speeder, to the driver who fails to signal, to the guys who rolls through the stop sign, to the driver who crosses the gore line.**

Seriously, isn't life like that?

Doesn't life sometimes feel so fast and out of control? Like life is one, big bumper car ride? Like no matter what we do, people are crashing into us and we're crashing into them? No wonder Shane thought that his life was, "Too good to be true." In the fast lane, it's only a matter of time before someone loses control and crashes. All you can do is just hope that they don't crash into you.

But even if your life's never in the fast lane, what makes you think you're immune to the forces of life? What happens to the guy in front of you *can happen to you*. That's the truth behind the wheel of life. We're all susceptible. Each and every one of us. That's the life we travel when we get into our cars each morning. We have no idea what we are about to face, yet the potential for problems hovers over us like a storm cloud. Sure, everything usually works out great. We get to work, home or our favorite vacation place in safety. But isn't that really why we all slow down and gawk at every accident scene that we pass? In no uncertain terms, that could be us.

I was stuck in traffic again just the other day. A two car accident had everyone on the highway creeping along. As I neared it, I saw that there was no reason to stop. They were obviously not hurt and were getting assistance on the cell. But just like everyone else, I slowed down and gawked at the scene. A man in his late forties, well dressed in suit and tie, was pacing around the front end of his smashed, luxury SUV. The girl he hit was younger, probably mid-twenties and by the looks of her car, didn't have the same financial resources as the man who hit her. As I slowly past them, the thought struck me, *Anyone, anytime, anywhere*. There is no rhyme or reason. Traffic is no respecter of persons. It doesn't care if you're rich or poor, good looking or ugly, married or single, young or old, religious or Atheist. It doesn't even care if you have a perfect driving record. If it doesn't get you today, there's no guarantee that it can't get you tomorrow.

So why is it that when we see an accident we slow down and think, *Man, that could have been me if I just left the house five minutes earlier,* but not when we pass other accidents in life? You know, accidents like the mangled scene of the guy on the corner with his cardboard sign, begging for money? Or the family down the block that is drowning in debt and feeling foreclosure breathe down their necks? Or the couple who desperately wants to have children but can't. Or the man whose spouse is struggling with depression and daily life is sometimes, well, just hard. Or the guy who found out that he has cancer and all the fears and unknowns that go along with that? And what about all those accidents that we see every night on every channel? The television is filled with stories about how life slammed into people, how people slammed into life and just how ugly those scenes are. But how is it that every one of us is willing and able to stop and help someone hurt in a car accident but we quickly turn our eyes from these things? Do we really think we're immune to these things ever happening to our lives?

But let's argue for a minute that maybe that's not true for you either. Maybe you are immune to all of those tragedies as well. Maybe life has been good to you so far. Maybe you're driving down the road of life in a military issue, bulletproof Hummer and are as safe as can be. But if nobody is doing everything right and everyone is breaking the law, could it be that *you* are your own worst enemy? What then?

Whether or not life slams into us, we have ourselves to deal with. We are not perfect. We make mistakes. We are inherently destructive. You give man a good thing and eventually he will ruin it. We find a good friendship and we take it for granted. We marry a good wife and we divorce her. We build a good company and we run it into bankruptcy. On a personal level, we ruin our own lives and leave a trail of victims in our wake. We may not murder but we hate certain people with passion. We may not rape women but we steal their worth and value with pornography. We may not hit the kids and kick the dog but we unload a days worth of stress on those innocent lives with our silence and attitudes. We may not snort, inject or smoke illegal drugs, pick up hookers or live out of a cardboard box but in many ways, our lives are often just as void and just as tragic.

Maybe psychiatrist, Karl Menninger had it right when he said, "We need criminals to identify ourselves with, to secretly envy and to stoutly punish. They do for us the forbidden, illegal things we wish to do." We love seeing the good guys win don't we? But secretly, don't you sit through those movies cheering for the bad guys as well? I know I do. Isn't it easy to identify with them? To understand their plight? Doesn't a part of you envy what they're doing? And if it wasn't for the stout punishment that goes along with it, wouldn't we be more likely to do all the forbidden, illegal things that we wish we could do? And if that's true, is it because that really, deep down inside, we're really just as much a criminal as the criminals?

The truth is that I've never contacted anyone on the street who ever hoped, ever aspired to or ever even thought their life would end up in the mess that it's in. No one. Not one prostitute, "john", drug addict, gang banger, wife beater, porn addict, homeless person or accident victim. But they all ended up there. Successful business men, loving wives, innocent children, even church leaders; all caught in the crosshairs of life. And at one point in their lives, they all must have thought that the thread that separated them from that kind of life was anything but fine too. But life slammed into them. They slammed into life. And that's when I meet them, when that thread finally snaps. When it seems like all hope is lost. When it seems like there is nowhere to turn. When it seems like no one is there to help.

There are not two sides to life where you can choose to either walk on the wild side or on some tamer, safer version of it. Life is the wild side. It's like the morning commute that can affect anyone, anytime, anywhere. And that means that you're a part of the wild side whether you like it or not. And if that's true, wouldn't you rather live, walk and drive through life bulletproof from it all?

Maybe you don't buy into any of this. Maybe what you've got going on is working for you. Or maybe you just don't think it's possible. And that's cool. But I suspect that there are some of you that are done buying into everything else that you've tried. I suspect that there are others of you, like Shane, where the uncertainty of tomorrow hauntingly lingers in the back of your mind. And I suspect that for many of you, life already hasn't worked out so well. It's hit you with all kinds of bullets and you feel as if it's standing over you, about to finish you off. And you need hope. Hope that there is a better way to live life. Well I propose that there is. But don't just take my word for it. Come and see for yourself.

---

* The nuns I saw weren't transvestites but they were driving a red Dodge Magnum. (See *Praise Habit*, by David Crowder).

** Gore lines are solid white lines, triangular in shape, usually placed at highway entrance and exit ramps. Crossing them is against the law.

3

BAD COP, NO DONUT

You are remembered for the rules you break.

-Douglas MacArthur

Fall 1995

I had just spent the last three years behind bars in federal prison. Going in, I had assumed it was a place of punishment and envisioned the old chain gang as they busted rocks with sledge hammers while wearing their black and white striped uniforms. But I soon learned that you can have just about anything on the inside of the joint as you can on the outside. And that just didn't seem like punishment to me.

On the lighter end of it, the convicts all had jobs, their own store, workout equipment, libraries, TV's, radios and visitation with their families. But on the darker side, convicts brewed their own alcohol or, "hooch" by stealing fruit and yeast from the dining hall and fermenting it by hiding it in the heat ducts. Crack, heroin, meth and pot were all smuggled in through the visiting room. They gambled to pass the time and even had their own "bookies" running the numbers.

They constructed crude tattoo guns and left distinctive green images on each others bodies. Often depicted were the spider web on the elbow or tear drop just below the eye and just like the outside, it was a permanent reminder of their entangled lives and horrible pain. Even sex, the heterosexual kind, was attainable behind bars. As the visiting room became over-crowded and understaffed, some cons would sneak into the restrooms with their female visitors. The worst was when the restroom was full and they snuck behind the vending machines. I felt horrible for the families that reported seeing it. Especially for the kids. As if that place wasn't bad enough.

And just like the other side of the fence, out on the streets, it was no place to walk around without some kind of protection. Housing fifteen hundred murders, rapists, bank robbers, kidnappers, gang members, dope dealers and the occasional mob boss and terrorist pretty much ensured that. No, survival here was no different than the street. That was unanimous. It just took another form. Being "strapped" no longer meant that you were carrying a gun. It meant that you were holding a shank.*

shank- n. any instrument or object sharpened into a weapon, usually constructed in a prison environment, either crudely or elaborately, designed to kill another human being by stabbing or cutting. *being shanked-* v. a bad day in prison.

Correctional officer. Guard. Hack. It was all the same. Whatever they called you, the job still amounted to ensuring that grown men, convicted felons, remained incarcerated. Some guys called it "glorified babysitting." But it was far more dangerous than that. We didn't wear body armor and didn't carry mace, a baton or any other weapon. If you played by the rules like a good little officer and didn't carry a personal knife (which was prohibited) you would be out gunned by any con strapped with a shank. There was no protection. We carried nothing more than keys to open the doors and radios to call for help. That's one disturbing thing I quickly realized; if the cons want to take the place, they can do it at anytime. And that vulnerability began to weigh on me day after day, year after year.

From a very young age I had my heart set on being a cop, not some prison guard. There were no cool TV shows or movies about guards. I never imagined that I'd be guarding grown men who were unable to follow the rules of society. I never imagined I'd be pacing the same cage as men that often behaved like wild animals. I never imagined that I'd be stuck in such a pathetic, upside down world of existence. But my dreams had been stalled in the long, drawn out hiring process of several police departments and this filthy, stench of a place is where I found myself waiting; not as a stepping stone to Copland but serving my own sentence, eight hour shifts at a time. The loud clank of those bars, as they slammed closed behind me, reminded me of that fact every day. At least the convicts knew when they were getting out of that God forsaken place. I had no idea how long I would be there. I wanted out. I wanted to do what I had always dreamt of doing.

Two years later

"Through these doors pass the finest police officers in the world."

One step under that sign somehow left the distinctive smell of prison in the past. For the first time in my law enforcement career, before I ever knew what it meant and before I ever received my department issued bulletproof vest, I felt totally and completely bulletproof.

Within just a few weeks of studies, the police instructor finally said, "Tomorrow, Group A will be at the firing range,

Group B will be on the driving pad and Group C will be on the mats for self defense."

The shooting and fighting didn't interest me that much. I had done plenty of training in both of those while at the prison. Tomorrow, I was in Group B and I couldn't have been more excited. All the best cop shows had car chases and I was going to get paid to learn how to do it.

The next day, I stood on the hot asphalt watching as the first recruits maneuvered their cars through the cone pattern. I wasn't nervous. This wouldn't be the first time that I pushed the limits of a car. As fast as they were pushing them, I had pushed mine further. In fact, just two months before I started the police academy, I had earned my sixth speeding ticket.

Even after I became a cop, my need for speed didn't subside. One night on my way to work I got pulled over by a cop known as, "Old 91."* I had seen him around but I hadn't been on the job long enough to know his nickname, let alone the reason behind it. Old Ninety One was an older, fit, gruff looking cop but was also one of the nicest you would ever meet. As he approached my window, I wasn't nervous like I used to be. I *was* a cop. He tipped his eyeglasses down and examined me over the top of them.

"On your way to work?" he asked, seeing me in full uniform.

"Yeah, sorry. I'm running late."

"Alright, be careful tonight."

I appreciated the warning, knowing full well that he could have written me a ticket if he wanted to but thought, *Yeah man, and you're slowing me down* as I sped off.

So, I've had a little trouble driving fifty-five. I'm working on that. *Wink, Wink.* But if police departments only hired saints, there wouldn't be any cops on the streets. The fact was, I felt comfortable behind the wheel and that day, on the police driving pad, I let it all hang out.

With the cone pattern set up, the objective was to maneuver the Ford Crown Victoria Police Interceptor through the course as fast as possible without knocking down the cones. Not everyone did that so well.

"Don't hit the cones!" The police instructors barked. "What if one of those cones was an innocent kid that you just ran over?"

I took the warning under advisement but knew full well that I could race around those little orange, cone shaped kids with ease. I dropped the gear shifter into drive and slammed the accelerator to the floor. The roar of the engine wasn't the most impressive that I'd ever heard but then again, it was a cop car and I was getting paid to thrash it. It really doesn't get much cooler than that. With each approaching turn and obstacle, I thoughtfully obeyed the academy instructors driving tips. *Hands at three and nine o'clock. Don't cross your hands. Shuffle steer. Coast into the curves. Accelerate out of them.* The car's weight lurched forward as I braked to a stop. I slammed the shifter up from the D to the R and the next few hundred feet were faster than I'd ever been before, in reverse.

What was once raw driving talent was now becoming a professional race car driver. With a gun. I recognized the adrenaline coursing through my veins and let it push out the last remaining thoughts of the past five years that I had just spent in federal prison. Those days were over. This was the start of a new life. A bulletproof life. Or so I thought...

The next day, with the adrenaline gone, I sat quietly in my seat for another classroom lecture. As the police instructor addressed the class, I noticed that he looked more like a cartoon character than a cop. *He reminds me of someone.* With his white disheveled hair, bushy eyebrows and matching mustache, I thought of who it was. *Yosemite Sam.* But what made him look even more cartoonish looking was the old revolver that hung off his belt. We of course, carried high capacity semi-automatics. *Who carries six-shooting wheel guns anymore?* Apparently Yosemite Sam. But as animated as he appeared, the seven stripes on his left forearm said that after thirty-five years on the job, he was still all business.

"Forget everything that you've ever scene on TV," he said as he held up a bulletproof vest.

That sucks. I've seen a lot on TV.

"This is not a guarantee that you go home at night." The instructor's seriousness raised a few levels.

"The bulletproof vest that you will be fitted for today will stop most handgun rounds. It will not stop rifle rounds. It will not stop a shotgun slug. It will not stop a knife from penetrating your chest cavity."

What did he just say about a shank to the chest? Now he had my full attention.

He continued, "It will not stop the concussive force of a baseball bat to your spine. It will not stop a bullet from penetrating your torso if you're hit between the panels. And it obviously won't stop a round from splitting your skull wide open. If you are shot, several of your ribs may shatter and you'll have difficulty breathing. If you are shot, there is a good chance that you'll still receive traumatic injuries to your heart, lungs and other vital organs. There is a chance that you may still die. Do not try to be the Lone Ranger or John Wayne out there. This vest is not a guarantee but it does save lives and it's what you have available, so make sure that you use it.

Man, I love the Lone Ranger and John Wayne. This wasn't stuff that I had hoped to hear.

"Most importantly, this vest will definitely not stop a bullet *if you fail to wear it*. Are there any questions?"

The classroom remained silent. We were all unsure of what, if anything, to ask.

I'd say that pretty much waded through just about all of the misconceptions I had about being bulletproof. Fiction made me to believe that cops get shot, they survive and they go on to the next scene with reckless abandon, often without ever completing one report. Reality is that cops get shot and die even while wearing their bulletproof vest. Reality is that those who do survive often have substantial injuries. Reality is that many of them deal with Post Traumatic Stress Disorder. Reality is that there is no guarantee. Reality is that police work is real, dangerous and nothing like the black and white cowboy movies that I grew up watching. Those cowboys that hid safely behind wood barrels for bulletproof protection were fiction. But then again, so were the endless rounds they shot from their six-shooters without ever reloading.

Knowing all of this, I still exited the police academy *feeling* bulletproof because I was wearing nearly ten pounds of body armor. But the streets were about to teach me through experience what the academy couldn't drive home to me intellectually.

No guarantee

A well trained, well experienced officer responded to a call of a fleeing robbery suspect and a high speed pursuit ensued. The suspect finally stopped the car, ran on foot and found a place to lay in wait. As Martin searched for the suspect, the quiet apartment complex where he was hiding was suddenly brought to life by the echoing sound of automatic gunfire. The suspect's rounds hit Martin's bulletproof vest. But it was no match against the AK-47. It penetrated Martin's vest just like my academy instructor told me that it would. As good a cop as Martin was, he didn't have a chance against that kind of high powered ammunition and he died right there on scene.

This time the truth hit closer. Danny had transferred over to our team from the Gang Unit or, " G.U." as they were known. He was arguably one of the best cops on the street. He had a real talent with the bangers and brought in more guns than anyone else on our team, ever. Danny was patrolling, "Blood Hill" which got its name in the early 90's when Blood gang members occupied that entire block of run down, crack infested apartments. Two bangers had just rolled off the hill and Danny stopped them. When the passenger reached into his jacket pocket, Danny assumed he had a stash of dope. Danny was wrong and got shot. Point blank. In the face. I'll never forget the hole in my gut that day as I raced to get there, having a feeling that it was Danny who was shot and knowing that he was probably going to die.**

Two cops were working a nightclub. Only this time when the blood flowed, it was a cop's and it didn't stop until the cop was empty. A Mexican National was causing problems and the cops escorted him out of the bar. Same story, different day. On his way out, he muttered in Spanish but none of it was understandable. It was a nothing deal for the wild side. Just like *La Jeringa* had been so many times. But this time the suspect came back. With a gun. And like the coward that he was, shot both of them in the back. The two cops never saw it coming. Ronnie's vest saved him. Eric wasn't as fortunate.

Real life police work is nothing like TV or the movies. There is no guarantee. There is no, "Take two." It's far more dangerous, much bloodier and more final than that. I just wish I could have applied that truth to my personal life.

Living like a rock star

How fast do cops drive? As fast as they want to. -Anonymous

There's something interesting that happens when you give a man a bulletproof vest. Even though it only protects him from bullets, and even that is not a guarantee, he starts to feel invincible towards everything. That is, until life reminds him otherwise.

I had been a street cop for two years. From day one, I worked the midnight shift. Detail One. At that time in my career, I started work when normal people were turning off the lights and laying their heads down on a soft pillow. It was a time when I arrived at roll call half awake and still tired from not getting enough sleep during the daylight hours. But it was also a time when I would be quickly brought back to life by heavy amounts of caffeine and by anticipating what the next eight hours of crime and darkness would bring. It was a time when I not only saw the realities of what put men behind bars but that I had the power to put them there, for life. It was a time when I was the strongest, fastest and toughest that I've ever been.

But it was also a time when I let that bulletproof persona bleed into every other aspect of my life. It was a time when I was more than a cop. It was a time when I thought I was above the law because I was the law. It was a time when I thought that I could do as I pleased and where the only difference between me and a rock star was the fact that I couldn't play the guitar. And that's where the danger came.

Once again, I had found myself at the beckon call of the engine's roar. Only this time, I wasn't in a police cruiser and I wasn't on duty. I was off duty, in a drop-top Mustang and I had been drinking. Cop life had sunk its grips into me. It somehow made me believe that I was bulletproof, not only from 9mm and .45's, but from everything else in life. It somehow made me believe that my bulletproof lifestyle on the job equaled some kind of guarantee in life. What I had was a lesson waiting to be learned. Little did I know, that just around the corner, there was a bullet waiting for me. A bullet that my vest could not stop.

As I turned onto a dark street, everything about life seemed perfect. Great job, great wife, great times, great wheels. I was feeling like Shane felt but without the lingering fear. At that point in my life, there was no fear. I pushed on the accelerator and felt the wheels grab the street under the torque of the engine as the road began to curve.

What I didn't know, in my bulletproof state of mind, was that two county cops were parked on the side of the road and just waiting for the next idiot to drive by. I never saw them in the darkness until it was too late. I roared past them and was nearly two blocks away when Jimmy looked back and said, "I think those were county cops."

Panic flooded my mind. It seemed too late to pull over, stop and explain myself. Besides, if they were county cops, I knew I wasn't going to catch a break like Old 91 gave me. I knew I didn't deserve one. I didn't know what to do. I had been drinking and now found myself in a predicament that so many of the people that I had stopped had once been in. I looked in the mirror. There weren't any red and blue lights filling the dark sky behind me. *They aren't coming. But just in case…*I stomped on the accelerator again.

My mind asked, *What are you doing?* And before I gave myself the decency of an answer, I slammed on the brakes, jumped out and ran. Just like a criminal. Any bulletproof feelings that I once had were instantly and completely gone. Then, in my uncertain, scared, altered state of mind, I made matters worse and I lied about it.

That one mistake could have cost me my job. But I still paid for it dearly, receiving a sixty day suspension, one year of probation, a $750 fine, 120 hours of community service, nearly $20,000 in lost wages and attorney fees and more than an ounce of humility.

The guarantee that I thought I could do whatever I wanted because I was a cop, because I was bulletproof, was no different than the rock stars I admired growing up who trashed hotels, lived fast and furious and seemingly did whatever they wanted to because of their fame and fortune.

And it blew up in my face just like it does to every rock star who's ever tried it. That was my life lesson learned. Rock star style. Pretty stupid, huh?

But what about you? You may not have ever felt bullet-proof because you walk out of the house wearing ten pounds of body armor, a pistol and a badge but what about your money, looks, talent, ability, health, power, or status? Have those things ever made you *feel* bulletproof, invincible or give you a sense of guarantee in life? I'm willing to bet they have.

Remember Harry Ellis in the movie *Die Hard*? Harry was the slick looking, slick talking employee of Nakatomi Plaza who thought that negotiating million dollar deals before breakfast meant that he was bulletproof. Harry should have asked *Die Hard* hero, John McClane if his success would make him bulletproof against a group of gun wielding, terrorist thieves. Maybe he would have shut his big mouth. Maybe he would have realized that success doesn't stop bullets and maybe, just maybe, villain Hans Gruber wouldn't have killed him.

But forget about the movies. What about real life people who believed they had real life protection against real life threats? Stuntman, Evel Knievel said, "I thought I was bullet-proof or superman there for awhile. I thought I'd never run out of nerve. Never." Hockey great, Brett Hull said, "You think you are invincible and then all of a sudden you think you are useless. It's the worst feeling I've had in my life." And country singer Johnny Cash said that as long as he had a few "bennies," he was guaranteed to hit the stage with the courage and confidence that he couldn't find without them.[1]

Harry had success, Evel had nerve, Brett had talent, John had drugs and I had a bulletproof vest, a badge and alcohol. And we all ended up in the exact same place. Wrong.

Because the truth is that money might protect you for awhile but what happens when it runs out? Success might protect you for awhile but what happens when you fail? Good health might protect you for awhile but what happens when you get sick or injured? And even when those things do work out, what happens when your money can't cure your disease? Or when your success can't save your child? Or when you're self medicating pills and alcohol aren't curing any of your problems? What happens then?

What happens is that we find ourselves standing in the storms of life, holding an umbrella that's all arms and no protection. And that's just not how life has to be. Our life can be bulletproof. It's not out of arms reach. It's not some fairy tale dream or fountain of youth, promising us what it can't deliver. It's attainable. We just have to sift through the misconceptions and deception that money, looks, talent, ability, health, power, status and even a bulletproof vest leave us with. Those *things* are just as vulnerable and unpredictable as what we're afraid to face. Those *things* all break, fail, and eventually wear out. Those *things* are mere camouflage when what we need is real protection. And when we trust in them to live a bulletproof life, the result is disappointment. Every time. Guaranteed.

So maybe what we need to start living a bulletproof life isn't some *thing* but simply a truth. Want to know what that truth is? That's next.

---

* "Old 91" got his nickname from only having nine fingers and one testicle.

** Remarkably, Danny didn't die. He was back on the job within three months and continued to stop gang bangers who were just as willing to shoot him.

4

MAN IN BLACK*

Fear is pain arising from the anticipation of evil.

-Aristotle

January 2006

I have been in hundreds of dangerous and potentially deadly encounters over the course of my career. I have always been prepared, always ready to act. Now, I found myself in trouble.

"Oh, my God, he's got a gun!" I warned Frank but it was too late. The barrel of the gun was already coming up on me. I did the only thing I could do. I unloaded on him.

Bam! Bam! Bam! Bam! Bam! Bam!

The sound of gunshots filled the alley, leaving a haze in the air and the smell of gunpowder in my nostrils. I felt the slide of my gun lock back. *Out of ammo.* I ducked for cover inside the car, looked at my weapon to verify it was empty and realized that now I was in serious trouble.

I had always heard that it would happen in slow motion. Not for me. For me, it all happened in fast forward. I went from being in a state of alertness into a state of complete unawareness and finally into a state of panic. Condition black. Everything I had learned, everything that I had been trained to do and everything that I had experienced had been disabled. Without my bulletproof vest, panic rushed in and flooded my mind. It wasn't so much looking at the wrong end of the barrel of a gun, it was knowing that I didn't have the time or the protection to stand there and take a hit. And I wasn't ready to lie in a dark, filthy alley, bleeding until I died. I had wished I'd worn my bulletproof vest.

Rewind

I had been assigned to the Narcotics Unit for training. This wasn't a shirt and tie kind of training. I've never really been a shirt and tie kind of guy. This was an undercover assignment that mainly focused on narcotics and prostitution. "Dope and whores," as they call it.

We were conducting a buy-bust operation targeting street level drug dealers. The plan involves an undercover cop, or UC, finding a dealer, buying some dope and walking away. He then gives the bust signal and uniformed officers immediately roll in and make the arrest. Thus, the buy and the bust.

With only two hours left in the shift, we were looking to make one deal and go home for the night. The undercover would make the deal and the uniforms would make the bust. Nothing special. Same thing, different day. As we briefed for the operation, the sergeant reminded us of the fact that because it was late and dark, the suspect's perception of escaping would be higher and the likelihood that he would probably run was exponential.

While domestic violence calls are dangerous, foot chases are probably the most dangerous thing a cop encounters. They are fluid, can escalate quickly and often leave us at a disadvantage. While we have the time to de-escalate most other situations, foot chases force us to adapt to a quickly changing terrain with quickly changing circumstances. Additionally, most criminals know the area far better than we do and even though there may not be any presence of a weapon at the onset, that doesn't mean they don't have one. Cops make assumptions, complacency sets in and the result is a deadly combination.

The stakes get raised if you lose sight of the suspect during the chase. Crooks will often lay in wait, just like the one who had killed Martin. They either hide or ambush you if the opportunity arises. Regardless of how it turns out, when you lose sight of a suspect, the hunter becomes the hunted and it becomes a win-win situation for someone with their back against the wall.

Then there's the act of actually catching the suspect. Often times, it's a one-on-one fight until your backup arrives. One minute fighting with someone who has nothing to lose seems like a million years. And as a cop, you have to remember there is always at least one gun involved in every fight, yours. That leaves the perp fighting for his freedom and the cop for his life. Hundreds of cops have been killed in the line of duty from bullets fired from their own weapon. And of course, none of this takes into account, "the dope factor." Every well trained, physically fit cop is at a disadvantage against a suspect hopped up on crack, meth, LSD or PCP.

Those were all factors nestled deep within my mind that would be the catalyst for my first shooting. But despite all those factors and even though the department had issued me a bulletproof vest free of charge, I wasn't wearing it. As an undercover officer, no one was. When I think back about it now, I remember that police instructor's bushy eyebrows as they rose up and he reiterated his point, "This vest will definitely not stop a bullet *if you fail to wear it*." Hindsight is always 20/20.

Had we read the warning signs, maybe this whole operation would have been scrapped. Earlier that hour, within blocks of our target location, several shots had been fired outside a bar. No suspects. No victims. Not related to our deal. Operation was a go. Detectives then checked out another location where we would attempt to make a buy but noticed five marked police cars handling a robbery where the victim had been pistol whipped. Dangerous night. But this was Detroit Avenue and "dangerous" was standard operating procedure. They simply moved the operation another two blocks and everything was back to go.

What's the saying? Third time's a charm?

With our undercover officer wired up and our surveillance and arrest teams in place, the UC got out and started walking Detroit Avenue looking for the dope man. Another detective was listening to the transmitter and relayed what was happening to us over the radio.

"Okay. The UC is out..."

It wouldn't take long to find the dope man. It never did on Detroit Avenue. Less than five minutes later...

"He just hooked up with a black male in the 1200 block of Folsom Street..."

"Light colored hoodie, blue jeans."

"They're talking."

"Standby...He wants him to trip with him."

"Trip." The dealer wanted to take the UC somewhere else to make the deal. Warning flag. The possibility that they were going to rob our UC just went up dramatically.

I had positioned myself where I could see the whole deal going down. Suddenly, two other men walked up. No big deal...maybe. But maybe one of them was holding the dope. Maybe one of them was holding the cash. Maybe they were the, "muscle." Either way, we now had multiple suspects until we determined otherwise. Another warning flag. The ante was going up quickly. Way up.

Then just like that, the UC had it in his hand. Forty dollars worth of crack cocaine.

"Okay, it's a bust. It's a bust."

Someone was now looking at State Statute 18-18-405: Unlawful Distribution, Manufacturing, Dispensing, Sale or Possession of a Controlled Substance. A Class 3 Felony. Punishable by Four (4) to Twelve (12) Years and/or $3,000 to $750,000 fine [5 years mandatory parole].[2]

The UC had made the deal, gave the pre-arranged bust signal and was now walking away. The most important part of the operation was a success; our undercover was safe. Now for the fun stuff. Time to catch our crook.

Two undercover cars slowly started moving in. The uniforms are there to make the arrest but we always have plain clothes officers closer to the action to make sure our UC remains safe and to keep an eye on the suspect. I began to move in from my own surveillance location but got stopped by a red light.

Eagerly waiting for the light to change, I watched as a uniformed car pulled onto the block to make the arrest. They were still about a half a block away from the suspect. I knew that if the suspects saw them before they could get close enough to make the arrest, the chase was on. This still had the potential to go bad. The light turned green and I stomped on the accelerator. I knew he was going to run. I could feel it. I had seen it all before and my gut was telling me it was going to happen again. I could almost feel the adrenaline coursing through my veins in anticipation for the dangerous foot chase that was just waiting to happen.

Stop

To better understand this story, you have to know what I know. In the academy, they taught us something called an, "awareness spectrum."[3] The instructors used a color scale to provide you with an early warning system for any given threat. Simply stated, it's where your head should be while playing The Game. Understanding it is critical. But understanding why it's critical is just as important. Because if you are not prepared to act, you cannot act appropriately and if you cannot act appropriately, people get hurt.

Here then, is wisdom of The Game.

First there's Condition White. Simply put, your mind's not in the game. It is the level to avoid at all costs. It's a state of mind where you're not focused on the job or the dangerous environment that you're in. Your mind is thinking about things it shouldn't be. For cops, it's a mental condition that you can't afford to spend any length of time in. Your life and the lives of the people around you depend on it. Complacent cops live in condition white. They assume everything will turn out fine, like it did on the last call and don't take what they're doing seriously.

The next level is Condition Yellow. It's a relaxed state of mind but one that's ready to go at any second. This is the mentality that athletes operate in on the field and the one that you want to operate in on the street. It's a constant evaluation process. Without acting paranoid, you simply take in every thing around you. That mentality makes you aware of potential dangers and how to deal with them appropriately if the need arises. On patrol, when I drive by cash accepting businesses like gas stations or convenience stores, I look through the front windows watching for indicators of the robbery that will eventually happen. When it does, I want to see it. I don't want to be caught off guard. Condition Yellow makes cops wonder, "What if?" What if a gunman did rob the store as I drove by? What would I do? How would I handle it? It only takes a second to happen and you better be prepared because a second will change your life.

Good cops operate in this level even while off duty. No matter where I am, I find myself mentally sizing people up, determining what it might take to win a fight with them, looking at their clothing for weapons, watching the doors at public places or just running through possible scenarios in my head. That conditioning makes people think cops are paranoid. It's not that we're paranoid; it's just that dealing with the worst of the worst in a job that has the potential to kill you every minute of every day just forces you to look at the world, your life, and everything in it, a little differently.

Condition Orange is when the bells and whistles start going off. Something is definitely wrong with the picture. You evaluate your available tactics and are focused to the point of knowing exactly what appropriate action you're going to take if necessary.

Condition Red. What was a defensive mentality has now become an offensive action. The situation demands your immediate response and you act.

And finally, Condition Black. Condition Black is an awareness disaster. It's a situation where you were caught thinking in Condition White when a deadly force encounter emerged. Your mind cannot ratchet up appropriately or quickly enough to handle the situation. Panic is upon you and overtakes you. The situation is past your control and you either respond inappropriately or not at all. Either way, the result is often serious injury and/or death.

Resume play

I was in Condition Yellow, right where I was supposed to be. I was ready and alert for our operation and the ensuing foot chase. I knew that if the suspects were to run, they would most likely run east between the houses. The other detectives had the north covered and the uniforms had the south covered. Both blocked the west and it was an unlikely route of escape anyways, as the suspect would have too much ground to cover crossing the street. No, if the suspect ran, it was going to be east; through the houses, into the dark and into his territory. And if he was going to run, I needed to beat him into position to have the safest advantage to assist our uniforms in apprehending him safely.

I turned off Detroit Avenue and into the alley but I had to stop abruptly. Two men were walking on the sidewalk, about to cross the alleyway and I didn't see them until the last second. No big deal. The first guy walked past the front of my car and I started to continue on. I ramped up Condition Yellow to Condition Orange. I was getting mentally prepared for this dope arrest to become a foot chase. But as I drove by, the other guy kicked my car and I heard a loud, "Whack!"

I don't know why I stopped. I should have cared less and just kept going. Maybe it was the cop in me. But either way, I stopped and got out of the car to see if there was any damage and to deal with him if there was. Without thinking about it, my mind dropped gears to Condition White over this minor, unrelated traffic altercation.

The next five seconds seemed to occur in a millisecond. I was completely and utterly unprepared for what was about to happen. As I opened the door, I identified myself as a cop, lifting the badge that was hanging around my neck so it was visible. But he was already closing ground on me as he approached quickly and aggressively. He yelled something (inaudible) as he reached down with his left hand and pulled up his shirt. Panic overtook me. I knew what was about to happen. My worst fear was about to come true.

That's when I saw it. Just before his right hand grabbed hold of it. It was the butt of a pistol sticking out of his waistband. My eyes became fixated on it. It was all that I could focus on. I felt frozen in panic. *This can't be happening.* As he began to draw the weapon, I saw the barrel clear his waistband as he started to draw down on me.

It's amazing how fast your mind can gather, analyze and process information. As I watched all this unravel in front of me, I knew that I didn't have my bulletproof vest on. I knew that if he shot me, there was a better than average chance I was going to die that night. Because of the narrow alley, I knew I didn't have any avenue of escape. I knew that if I didn't respond in the same aggressive manner as the person who was intent on shooting me was, I was a dead man.

I had been prepared to go one step up from Condition Orange to Condition Red with the dope deal if need be. But now I was faced with a situation of having to go from Condition White to Condition Red. Three separate thought processes. Not a good thing. Not possible in the time given. The result? I went Condition Black.

I managed to react by ducking just low enough to get some kind of protection behind my car. I knew it wasn't the best cover but hoped that it would prove to be enough in the pinch I was in. Then I unloaded my backup gun in his direction. Six rounds of .380 caliber ammunition. It was nothing better than Yosemite Sam's old wheel gun that I once joked about. Meanwhile, Frank had rolled out the passenger side and fired several rounds at the suspect as well.

In this unexpected, frantic shootout, one of my rounds hit the rear window post of my car. The other rounds are debatable as to whose gun they came from. One round apparently went through a bus as it drove westbound on Detroit Avenue. One round hit the side of a church building several blocks away and one round had ricocheted into the leg of the non-combatant friend. To my knowledge, the other seven rounds went unaccounted for. I just thank God they didn't find their way out the barrel of our guns and deal an innocent victim a hand of, "Aces and 8's." The dead man's hand.

When I came back up from the cover of the car and realized that I was out of ammo, the suspect was gone. That's when Condition Black really took hold of me. I didn't feel any pain. My training told me that I probably wouldn't just yet, the adrenaline wouldn't allow it. But I was sure that I had been hit. My mind was in complete and utter survival mode. I didn't know where the suspect was but at that moment I didn't care. The panic suddenly felt cold and immobilizing, like I fell through the ice and into the freezing waters of a lake. I felt my chest for bleeding and reluctantly looked at my hand.

No blood, my eyes communicated to my mind and I took a deep breath of relief.

I ran over to Frank to see if he was alright. He assured me that he was and called it out, "Shots fired. Shots fired. Suspect male is running east bound, north of Detroit Avenue."

Cops flooded the area and the suspect was caught shortly thereafter, remarkably unharmed.[**] While most gunfights occur at a staggering short distance of about seven feet, I was still amazed to know that our suspect escaped a hailstorm of bullets, even at more than twice that distance. It was still unbelievably close. I suppose the biggest reason that he wasn't shot dead in the alley that night is because neither Frank nor I ever saw it coming. Had we anticipated any kind of confrontation, been bulletproof and mentally prepared, two expert marksmen would have surely left him dead.

But that thought didn't make my panic go away. At headquarters, before the post shooting interview, panic overtook me again and my mind would not accept the truth that I had not been shot. *Maybe I was hit when I turned to take cover and no one noticed.* I calmly walked past several command staff to the bathroom then frantically yanked my shirt up and looked at my back in the mirror. I was unharmed but I didn't feel that way.

Six hours later, I stepped through the back door of our home. It was eight o'clock in the morning and I had now been awake for nearly twenty-four hours with the stress of the shooting still weighing on me. I didn't make it three feet before my wife was in my arms and crying. It was obvious that she hadn't slept either. As she finally went up to bed, I felt a sharp pain in my shoulder. My mind panicked again. I didn't want her to know what I was thinking and told her that

I would be up in a minute. I went into the bathroom, looked myself over for a third time and wondered how long these panic attacks were going to last.

The truth of it all

Despite how incapable *things* had always been at making my life bulletproof, it took that one moment of *not being bulletproof* to finally wade through all the misconceptions and deception that I had ever believed. The truth is that being bulletproof doesn't mean that I won't get shot, won't get hurt and can't die. It doesn't mean that I am invincible. It certainly doesn't give me any guarantees. It doesn't mean that I won't make mistakes along the way. I can assure you that I will. The simple truth is that being bulletproof merely *enables me* to do what I was designed to do. That's it. Nothing more, nothing less.

It enables me because it does for me what I cannot do for myself. Do you see? My body is incapable of stopping bullets. But a bulletproof vest is capable of stopping them. Therefore, by wearing a bulletproof vest I become enabled by its power. And that protection is what enables me to do what I was designed to do, to protect and serve. The same is true with a seatbelt. No matter how much we may brace ourselves for impact, we are incapable of protecting ourselves in an accident. But a seatbelt is capable of protecting us by limiting our body's motion. Therefore, by wearing a seatbelt we become enabled by its power. And that protection is what has enabled so many people to do what they were designed to do. To live.

So with that principle as a reference, I offer you the truth you've been waiting for. A truth that has the power to enable you against all of life's threats. A truth that will allow you to do what you were designed to do. A truth that is waiting for you just around the corner...

---

    * A reference to my favorite recording artist, Johnny Cash.

    ** The suspect had been released from prison and was on parole for 2nd degree assault. He had a four page rap sheet including numerous assaults and a weapon charge. He plead guilty in a plea bargain agreement and went back to prison.

5

SPEED LIMIT 55
Part one

*The best car safety device is a rear view mirror
with a cop in it.*

-Dudley Moore

I'll officially confess it. I can't drive fifty-five. I can't. That is unless, maybe, I'm driving through my neighborhood. Nope. I take that back. I cannot do it.

I know, you're probably thinking, "But aren't you a cop?" Hey, I'm trying to be real here, give me a break. At least let me tell you why. It's not the speed or the thrill. I've had both, with full lights and siren and its like anything else, it becomes routine. No, I speed for the same reason that I eat too fast. I'm impatient. Going from point A to point B is just another necessity of life for me and the longer it takes, the less time I have for more important things, like...um, things. Ok, I can't think of anything specifically but believe me, I've got things to do. Speed limit? I could probably save five days of my life if I just drove a little faster each day.

See? I don't have time for that. I need those five extra days. I've got things to do.

Knowing that, don't start pointing fingers.

"See? The cop is speeding, why can't I?"

First of all, stop tattling. It's so juvenile. Secondly, do as I say and not as I do. And third, quit pointing. The cop might see me.

Sometime in your own past

But you probably know the feeling. You look into your rear view mirror and see the red and blue lights flashing behind you. Your heart rate immediately spikes as you glance down at the speedometer. Your mind frantically tries to remember what the last posted speed limit sign was and try to calculate just how fast you were driving over it.

Seventy-two minus...um...sixty-five, I guess....is...um... seven. Seven over. Okay, that's not too bad....

Don't lie. If you were speeding, that's how it went down. If your subtraction was right and it was only seven miles over the speed limit rather than the infamous, ticket producing double digits, maybe you can talk your way out of it. That is unless; you were speeding intentionally, in which case there is no need to try and remember the last posted speed limit sign because you definitely know that it was fifty-five miles per hour and there is no reason to solve any math problems because you've already calculated it. And therefore, while you're still nervous, its obvious that your mind is not working on the solution to a math problem and you, my little friend with the need for speed, are definitely not getting out of your ticket.[*]

The cop comes up to your window and asks you for your driver's license, registration and insurance. You dig through your over stuffed glove box, thumb through your paperwork and eventually hand over each piece of documentation, feeling somewhat like a foreigner in an occupied country.

"Did I do something wrong officer?"

Now really, isn't that the dumbest question, even if you were speeding unintentionally? You know that he didn't stop you to congratulate you on your wonderful driving. You know that he didn't stop you out of sheer boredom. Of course you did something wrong. You know that. The "Man" isn't going to waste his time with you if you didn't. He's got quotas you know.** What you're doing is trying to get your money's worth out of some lame, three-credit, college psychology course that you had to take to graduate, hoping to create a miniscule amount of doubt in his mind that you were in fact not speeding. Reverse psychology. We get it. It doesn't work.

Behind the mirrored sunglasses and cheesy mustache, he answers your question with a question, "Do you know how fast you were going?"

This definitely isn't going how you had hoped. Now you know that he knows you *were* speeding. Duh! And he knows that you probably know exactly how fast you were going. His question of, "Do you know how fast you were going?" gives you;

1) The chance to admit your mistake, to show remorse, and to depend on his mercy, or
2) In the event you do not choose option #1, the opportunity to hang yourself with your answer.

You're hesitation and stuttering answer gives you away immediately. You have chosen to go with option #2 thinking you can play it off innocently.

"Um...sixty-five...I think."

Good answer. Not. If indeed you were driving sixty-five and the posted speed limit is fifty-five, then you just admitted to doing ten over. And if the speed limit is sixty-five, then why are we are having this conversation? Last I checked it's not illegal to drive the speed limit and that's why he's still standing there looking at you. *Yeah, this one looked like he would choose #2.*

You're wondering why this suddenly feels like a murder investigation.

Now he drops it on you like a well placed bomb, "You were doing seventy-two in a fifty-five. That's seventeen miles per hour over the posted speed limit, boy."

Fifty-five? No way. It must be a speed trap. That can't be good. And did he just call me boy? He doesn't look old enough to even carry a gun.

You should have gone with option #1.

I don't know what seventeen over the posted speed limit amounts to where you live, but in this city, it's a $160 fine and four points against your license. And I don't care who you are or how much money you have, a hundred and sixty dollars for a speeding ticket just plain sucks. Not to mention the points.

You watch him as he walks back to his patrol car, gets in and immediately starts writing.

God, please don't write me a ticket. Please, please, please.

The first reaction to a traffic stop is always that math equation but the second reaction is always prayer, whether you realize it or not, and for some reason it always seems to include three "pleases." As if those extra two are going to help.

You know you deserve a ticket but you're still hoping that maybe he'll come back with a warning or something. Yeah, right.

You wait. And wait. And wait. *What is he doing back there?* Guilt has turned to irritation and now you're just ready to get what you deserve and get on your way.

The cop finally walks back to your car, tips his glasses down and lays it on you. "Here's your license, registration and insurance back."

You shake your head, knowing what's coming.

He hands you the yellow copy of the ticket and says, "It's a $160 fine and four points against your license."

Yep, there it is. I knew he was writing me a ticket back there. You accept it and sit there staring at it. *Man, I don't have the money for a speeding ticket right now...and why is he still standing there?*

You sheepishly look up into those mirrored sunglasses and see your reflection. A smile spreads across his face as he hands you a handful of twenties. "Today's your lucky day. I'm going to pay that ticket for you. Now slow down. And have a nice day."

What? What the...is going on?

Your mind cannot even contemplate what is happening. You glance around. The cop's gone. You don't see the Candid Camera crew jumping out. You pinch yourself, assuming it's all a weird dream. *Ouch, not a dream.* Everything around you is still in color. *Can't be the Twilight Zone.* You are forced to make the only logical determination that your mind can make. *Holy...cow! That prayer stuff really works!*

----

* For the record, I don't write speeding tickets. I've never even used a radar gun.

** We don't have quotas. We can write as many tickets as we want.

6

SPEED LIMIT 55
Part two

If the ride is more fly, then you must buy.

-Snoop Dogg

In my new understanding of the truth surrounding a bullet-proof life, I had found the answer. But it wasn't just another *thing* that I found to enable me against life's threats, it was someone. If you truly want to live a bulletproof life, then let me introduce you to that cop who just stopped you.

It's not Mayberry's, Barney Fife. I don't think Sheriff Andy ever even let him drive. It's not that silly Hazard County Sheriff, Roscoe P. Coltrane. He couldn't catch the Duke boys; I doubt if he could catch anyone giving him a run for his money. It's not California Highway Patrol Officers Jon Baker and Officer Francis Llewellyn 'Ponch' Poncherello, even though they could catch you on those Kawasaki 1000's. And it's not Adam 12 partners, Pete Malloy or Jim Reed; although they might just be the only two cops nice enough to actually do it. Nope. You know who I'm talking about.

That cop is Jesus Christ.

Wait. Before you put this book down, let me assure you that this isn't about trying to get you to join some religion. I personally hate religion. Jesus did too. This is simply about introducing you to someone who can make your life bullet-proof, the only way it's really possible. From the inside out. What you do with it is totally and completely up to you. No sales, no pressure. In fact, if you don't like the fact this is what this book is about, skip the rest of this chapter and just read the rest of the cop stories. Seriously.

But if you're at least curious how Jesus Christ could make you bulletproof, then let's review what we know up to this point. We know that eventually life is going to hurl some pretty big bullets at all of us at some point in our lives. We know that the thought, "What if I was bulletproof," is a hopeful answer to those threats. And we know that the things we thought would make us bulletproof don't. But we also know that if we had something to enable us, something to do for us what we cannot do for ourselves, then maybe, just maybe that hope of a bulletproof life is still possible. So knowing that, let me propose the ultimate, "What if" question to you.

(Drum roll please)

What if...everything between you and God was cool?

"What? What do you mean?"

You know, cool. Like God wasn't mad at you for speeding. Like he actually forgot about all the other times he caught you speeding. Like God actually liked you and you actually liked him back. That kind of cool.

I'm proposing the audacious idea that if you allow God to pay your ticket, everything between you and God will be cool and your whole life will be bulletproof.

Is it a guarantee that life won't slam into you? No.

Is it a guarantee that you won't face pain, illness, suffering, financial difficulty, broken relationships or even death? Nope.

Is it a guarantee that life will be easy? Not at all.

It's a promise that the God of the universe will be with you when life is hard and more importantly, that you will be with him when all of that no longer matters. That's the bulletproof life.

So, if having that hope sounds like a better way to live your life and makes you want to know more, then let me give you the short version first because over the past two thousand years we sure have complicated a very simple message. A bulletproof life, in one sentence, is this: Our mistakes drove us away from God, but he pursued us, paid our ticket and enabled us stand before the judge, completely innocent.

That's it.

Pretty fly, huh?

Want to know more? Check it out.

The mistake and what it means

For the sake of an argument, let's assume that the only mistake you've ever made was blowing through that 55 mph zone at seventy-two miles per hour. Now, the actual mistake may not have been that big of a deal but it's what the mistake did to you. When you eventually stand in front of the judge to face the consequences of your mistake, you find that it separated you from the judge's good grace. You're no longer the good, innocent citizen that you once were. You're now a criminal. A traffic criminal albeit, but still a criminal. You broke the law and he has no choice but to punish you.

He asks you, "How do you plead to the speeding charge of driving seventy-two in a fifty-five?"

"Guilty."

"How then do you plead to Being Perfect in the First Degree?"

You've just admitted that you were guilty for speeding, you're only response to Being Perfect in the First Degree can only be the same. Sad day for you. The perfect life that you've lived up to now is over. Now the punishment.

As the judge looks over your once perfect driving record he says, "I hereby sentence you to death."

What? I know it felt like a murder investigation, but I was only doing seventeen over. It's not like I killed someone!

You may not have killed anyone but God says that our mistakes, any mistakes, are called sin. And you don't have to be a murderer, rapist or drug dealer to be a sinner. To God, one selfish, prideful moment is just as bad. And regardless of how "small" our sins are or how few of them we commit, God's punishment for them is all the same. That's what the sin did to you. It separated you from God's good grace. It gave you a death sentence.

We shout, "That's not fair!"

And if we were in a city, state or federal courthouse, we'd be right. That's not fair. But in God's courtroom it is fair. It's fair because God is perfect, pure and sinless. It's fair because we're not. It's fair because in light of those facts, we don't deserve to be hanging around with God for eternity. We can never be good enough, have enough or give enough. It's just not possible. Not for the Pope, Mother Theresa, Gandhi, a monk, your priest or you or me. The perfect God says that we can't be around him even if we've only made one mistake. The perfect God says that we have to be separated from his good graces, just like the judge in our story. The only difference is that with God, that separation is a spiritual one. You know, like hell.

Let me give it to you in a different way. Last year I found myself standing in a pile of trash at the county landfill. It was hot, dusty and the smell was horrific. A suspect had confessed to a murder and said that he had disposed of the body in a dumpster before fleeing the state. Apparently, the landfill keeps track of where incoming trash comes from and our detectives were able to narrow down a section of the landfill that they believed contained the deceased's remains.*

Cops were then assigned to sift through the trash in hopes of finding the body, because as far as most homicide trials go, it's *Corpus Dilecti*. Rough Latin translation, "No corpse, no case." Bottom line, we needed a body. Fortunately, I was only assigned there one day. But that was one long day. I can't count the times that I nearly vomited at the stench that I was standing in.

As the day went on, I watched as a cop sifted through the trash and lifted a porn mag from the pile that he was searching through. Now, I'm not pointing fingers or saying that I've never looked at porn, I'm saying that as I stood there watching him thumb through it, it hit me. *This is the condition we're in.* Whatever pretty little picture we've painted for ourselves about our mistakes and our own sin is dead wrong. Literally. No matter how small our mistakes are, they put us in the middle of absolute filth, the only thing we can breathe is stench filled air and as we stand there, we are literally dying; rotting away into the mess that we are standing in, one unstoppable second at a time. And when you truly understand that's the situation that you're in, you want nothing more than to get out of that mess as fast as possible.

Still with me? That's the bad news. Thankfully, there is a way to get out of that mess. So let me tell you just how good the good news really is.

The pursuit

I'm sure that most people know the basic story of Jesus. He was born from a virgin named Mary, lived a sinless life, died on a cross and rose from the dead. Arguably, much of the world believes that story. But I wonder if they understand what all of that really means.

When I was a boy, I remember a time when my mom was driving. On that occasion, I distinctly remember her looking up to see the stopped traffic in front of us. Life was about to deal us a blow that we weren't ready for. Not wearing seatbelts at the time, she gasped and put her arm across my chest as I shoved my arms into the dashboard, bracing for the impact. Thankfully, she stopped short and we never did crash. But think about that. A vehicle traveling at even thirty miles per hour still delivers thousands of pounds of force. About 4,800 pounds of force actually. That's about two and a half tons or the equivalent of dropping a two-hundred pound weight on your pinky toe. It's not even remotely possible that neither she nor I could have reduced personal injury to ourselves with either of those techniques. It takes the seatbelt, an outside force, to do what we are incapable of doing for ourselves. It's the same thing that my bulletproof vest does for me now. And that's what Jesus Christ does for us.

The good news is that Jesus jumped into the middle of that rotting mess we were standing in. He jumped in because we were incapable of jumping out. But just like it's not so much *the* sin but what the sin *did* to us, it's not so much that God jumped *to* you but *how* he did it.

When the bullet of sin was fired and it was barreling down on you to kill you, Jesus Christ stepped in the way. He became your bulletproof vest. Just like my bulletproof vest takes the damage so I don't have to, Jesus was damaged on our behalf. God, through his Son Jesus, placed himself between you and the deadly bullet of sin and in doing so paid your ticket that you were incapable of paying yourself. That's what the church calls grace and redemption.

The grace part is this: God did it because he chose to. Just like the police department favored my life and chose to provide me with a bulletproof vest. I didn't *deserve* it; I hadn't even stepped out of the academy yet. I didn't *earn* it; I hadn't even made one arrest. I couldn't *buy* it, it wasn't for sale. It was totally, completely and utterly free. It's the same with you and God. He chose you. He chose to give you what you don't deserve. He chose to give you what you cannot earn. He's not selling it, it's not for sale and you couldn't afford it if it was. He chose to buy it for you. It is God's gift to you out of his great love for you. That's the grace part and that's why so many people call it amazing.

The redemption part is this: He redeemed, or traded, his perfection for our sin. Because our sin still deserved to be punished. With death. So he was crucified. He did it, not only so that we wouldn't have to but because we couldn't. Our separation from God isn't a physical one, it's a spiritual one. When we physically die, our death cannot satisfy our own ticket of sin. If it did, that would mean that we all die and go to heaven. And I don't think anyone buys into that. No, Jesus Christ died because nothing was *perfect* enough to satisfy the penalty of our sin, except for him.

So understand this about grace; while God implanted this insatiable desire within us to make things right with him, it is not us who pursues God; it is God who pursues us. He follows along our life path and patiently waits for us to recognize our need for him and pull over. Not to spank us with an un-payable ticket but to offer us a better way to drive through this thing called life and to offer us a life that will last forever. And I'll bet that if you were to look back in the rear view mirror of your life, you'd begin to recognize the lights and siren of a God who was so desperately trying to get a hold of you.

In perfect standing

The good news gets better. Not only did the innocent (Jesus) choose to pay the ticket of the guilty (you and I) but Jesus Christ puts us in right standing with God. And that makes us perfect.

What? Perfect? I don't think so. I see imperfect "Christians" everywhere. What about that guy in my office? He says he's a Christian, but he's a jerk half the time. And what about that pastor who slept with that prostitute? He's definitely not perfect.

Religion often focuses on the fact that Jesus hung on a cross and paid our ticket but what it often misses what that means. It's not a guarantee that we won't get hit by life's storms. It's not a guarantee that we won't stumble along life's paths. It's not a guarantee that we won't screw things up and make more mistakes. It's not a guarantee that we *act* perfect. I think that's painfully obvious. But it does allow God to *see us as perfect.*

When we were driving our life in our own direction, God looked at us and saw our sin and the penalty that we owed. But when we stop, turn around and follow the guy who just paid our ticket, God begins to look at us through the perfect, protective lens of his own Son, Jesus Christ. What God once saw as guilty and damaged standing in front of him, he now sees as innocent and made right. He sees us as sinless and perfect, not because we are but because Jesus is. All of our mistakes, all our crimes, all our debts, all our sins…forgiven. Permanently. Forever. And that is what's perfect.

So that's it. That's the answer you've been waiting for. Jesus Christ paid your ticket and enabled everything to be cool between you and God, making you bulletproof from the eternal, spiritual death that was once inside of you.

But that's not the end. Jesus also enabled you to do what you were designed to do; to know the God of the universe for yourself and to have a personal, ongoing, interactive relationship with him. That's the bulletproof life. It's not a guarantee of the "good life." It's not a guarantee of life on Easy Street. It's a promise that you don't have to be alone when life slams into you like a .45 caliber to the chest or out of nowhere like a car wreck. And it's a promise that if it does, literally, that life still goes on. Forever. With God. In heaven. And if that ain't cool, nothing is.

It's all up to you

You might think that we would all jump up and down and shout, "Yes! That's incredible. I want that!"

But unfortunately, as easy as God has made it for us, that's often the hardest part, even though that doesn't make sense in any other area of our life. Someone offers us a gift and we accept it, even if it's useless.

"Oh...a space pen that writes upside down, uh, thanks. Just what I needed."

But how many of us would balk at the idea of taking the cops cash to pay our ticket? Is it because something about it just wouldn't feel right? Absolutely. A lot of people wouldn't accept it because it doesn't feel right. It doesn't feel right because we are forced to face our crime, our own mistakes and our own inadequacy, up close and personal. And it's ugly. It doesn't feel right because we know that we deserve to be punished. It doesn't feel right because in light of all that, we can't bring ourselves to believe that we could ever be viewed as perfect. It doesn't feel right because we don't understand or just can't accept that kind of grace. And because of all that, a lot of people don't.

"Guilty your Honor."

"Son, the fines been paid. The charges against you have been dropped. All you have to do is accept it."

"No your Honor, I insist."

People insist on driving in their own direction, even if that means driving right off the edge of a cliff. And if that's the choice you make, God won't stop you.

"What? That doesn't sound like a good God. If he loved me, he should stop me."

But that is what makes him a good God. He offers the same bulletproof life to everyone but he doesn't force it on anyone. It's just like a judge who won't force you to plead innocent if you stupidly choose to plead guilty. Yes, he wants you to choose him. Yes, he taps your shoulder, tugs at your heart and places warning signs all around you. Yes, he is hoping that you'll stop what you're doing for a minute and just see that what he has for you is a better way to do life, both now and forever. God is good. He's so good that he gives you that choice. No sales, no pressure, just a choice.

In one parking spot is everything the world has to offer you. Money, looks, talent, ability, health, power, status, success. And if those are the components of the life that you want to drive, then don't just drive them off the lot. Drive them like you stole them and don't ever look back. God's only question is, "How's that working out for you?"

Because parked next to all of those things are what God has to offer you. Payment for all of your mistakes, right standing with the Judge, peace during the storms of life that the world can't offer and a promise of an eternal life after this temporary one is over. And if that's the life you want to drive, take Snoop Dogg's advice and buy into it. Because it's the most fly ride that you'll ever find. Guaranteed.

The only thing is that you can't drive them both. That's one thing Jesus made very clear. They'll take you into two totally different directions. So, think it through. Weigh the decision out for yourself. And remember, this is a no sales, no pressure offer that God has for you. What you do with that offer is totally and completely up to you.

But for me, it's a no-brainer. I tried driving what life had to offer me. And I definitely drove it like I stole it. And it still got me nowhere. So now, I'm driving life God's way. In his direction. Following the guy that paid my ticket. And life has never been better. But don't get me wrong. That doesn't mean it's easy. It's often as difficult as an American driving through England. And that's really what Part Two of this book is all about. Relearning to live and drive this new found life that God has given me. But I think you'll find, as I have, that it's also the best life you could have ever imagined.

---

* The search for the dead body had been going on for months. When I arrived, the first thing I noticed was the horrific smell. But the second thing I noticed were the American flags those cops before me had risen from the rubbish. There, in the worst place I've ever been, Old Glory still danced in the wind as she had for so many others in the worst places they had ever been. It was, and may always be, the most patriotic sight I'd ever seen.

7

POLICE TACTICS
A better way to be bulletproof

Sometimes I am two people.
Johnny is the nice one. Cash causes all the trouble.
They fight.

-Johnny Cash[*]

Here are some of the calls for service that we get and the general consensus that cops have about them: Domestic violence- Good call. Pretty good chance you'll get to beat a wife beater. Silent alarm- Bad call. Almost always false. Armed robbery in progress- Good call. May not get there in time, but the potential is exhilarating. DUI accident- Very bad call. Hate doing accident reports, DUI booking process is too long and complicated. Shooting, stabbing, suicide- All great calls. May not get to chase, arrest or shoot anyone, but the possibility of seeing blood and guts is cool. Naked man with an axe-[**] Good and bad call. Good chance this will be a great story to tell. Bad thought to have to see a naked man.

One night, I received one of those bad calls. The radio crackled.

Dispatch, "221?"

"221."

"On a silent alarm at 4394 Brooklyn Street."

"221 clear."

Dispatch, "Car to cover 221, 4394 Brooklyn Street on a silent alarm?"

"222, I'll cover."

Dispatch, "Thanks 222."

My first thought, *Bad call.*

I hadn't even been on the job for a year and was already bothered by the silent alarm call. I must have responded to nearly a hundred of them and every one was always false. Despite my bothersome attitude about those calls, I still never became complacent. Curiosity may have killed the cat but complacency kills cops. Complacency is for guys we call, "slugs" who would rather pick through a box of donuts than ensure they go home at night. And I was *Nolo Gastropodi.* Latin translation, "No slug."

The alarm location was at a large manufacturing building. I immediately assumed it was another false alarm. *Probably some cleaning crew member who forgot the code or accidentally tripped the alarm.* Either way, I hoped to clear it as quickly as possible and get back in service for the next good call.

As I got close, I blacked out the Crown Vic's lights, notified radio that I was Code 6 on scene and parked. My cover officer arrived right behind me.

"What's up, G?"

"Nothing. Tired. And I'm sick of these alarm calls. You?"

"I hear you. I'm dragging tonight too. Hey, I'll check the east side."

As I watched him walk away into the darkness, I heard him mumble his own thoughts about false alarms. I began to walk the fence line on the west side of the building and noticed an office with the light still on. As I got closer, I saw a man inside. He kept bending over and appeared to be picking up trash off the floor. *Cleaning guy.*

With the lights on inside and the darkness outside, he couldn't see me so I stood there behind cover and watched him for a minute. He was loading up the trashcan alright but not with trash. He was using it to carry all the stuff he was about to steal. *Sweet! A real live burglary in progress.*

I was more excited at the fact that it was finally a legitimate alarm than I was at the fact this was going to be a great call after all.

Unaware if he was armed or not, I proceeded with caution. I immediately radioed dispatch and advised her of what I had. I wanted the arrest but I also wanted my cover officers as close as possible had it gone south.

I climbed the eight foot chain link fence that surrounded the building and worked my way through the barb wire. After making it over the fence, I crept through the darkness, found some cover and laid in wait. As a responder, you don't get this kind of opportunity often, so I was going to take full advantage of it.

Matt was so far on the other side of the building that when I asked for cover another officer arrived first. He got out of his patrol car, looked at me, looked at the fence and said, "I can't get over that."

I just stared it him for a moment thinking, *Can't or won't?* As I sized him up, I thought that maybe he really couldn't. He wasn't a small guy. I mumbled, "Donuts" under my breath with the same grudging demeanor that Seinfeld always said, "Newman" with when referring to his overweight, obnoxious neighbor and turned my attention back to what I was clearly going to have to do all by myself.

Seconds later, I saw a long crack of light break the darkness as the exterior door opened and the suspect came out. He wasn't in any hurry. In fact, he was trying to balance so many items on top of the trashcan that it took both hands for him to carry it. *At least he doesn't have a gun in his hand.*

Twenty feet away, still concealed in the darkness and protected by the cover of the brick wall that I was hiding behind; I keyed my radio and whispered, "221."

"221, go ahead."

"221, the suspect just came out the west side of the building. He's coming right at me. Hold the air."

I didn't know what was about to come down and I didn't want some other rookie, or "boot" as we were referred to, jamming the air with useless information. My heart was pounding now. My mind raced through all of my, "tools in the toolbox." That was an academy term that basically meant that I had my voice, fists, feet, mace, baton and handgun at my disposal. Which "tool" I decided to use for a particular situation was up to me. I would just have to be able to articulate it to a grand jury and be Monday morning quarterbacked the rest of my life for the spilt decision I was about to make had I choose the wrong one. No pressure.

I decided on the foot strike. That was reasonable. I wasn't sure if he was armed or not, didn't want to give my position of cover away by announcing myself, decided that my mace or baton as a higher level of force wasn't necessary at this point and without a visible deadly weapon, my gun was not yet an option. Having played college soccer, I was pretty secure with the foot strike.

I watched him as he walked closer. Closer. I could picture William Wallace in *Braveheart,* telling me to, "Hold." My heart was pounding so hard now that I could hear it in the silent air. I knew that for this to work perfectly, I needed to see the whites of his eyes before I engaged him. And since it was nearly pitch dark that was going to be close. When he was practically on top of me, I stepped out of the darkness and placed the tread of my boot smack dab in the middle of the stolen items he was carrying, kicking with everything I had. The items went airborne, he fell to the ground and I had him handcuffed faster than a junkie can say, "Crack."

Glancing to my right, I saw donut boy still standing on the other side of the fence.

"Thanks for the cover," I muttered sarcastically, half hoping he heard me and half hoping he didn't.

I love that story. I love it for how the whole arrest went down, for the fact that donuts actually put me in jeopardy and for utilizing all five of the most basic police tactics. Those tactics are; invisible deployment, restraint, distance, cover and surprise.[4] And while actually utilizing all five of those basic tactics on one call doesn't happen very often, on this call I was able to arrive without the bad guy knowing I was there, get backup even though he couldn't climb the fence to help me, keep a safe distance away until necessary, use the building for additional protection and give him the biggest surprise he'd probably ever had.

But as important as those tactics are, we don't use tactics *to make us bulletproof.* We use tactics because they're a *better way to be bulletproof.* That's why Sgt. Esterhaus from *Hill Street Blues* reminded his cops to be careful before every shift. Sure they were bulletproof but that doesn't mean you put your protection to the test unnecessarily.

Be big, bad and bulletproof but be big, bad and bullet-proof better. Try saying that five times fast.

So what does all this have to do with the bulletproof life that we're talking about? Everything. We come to this point in our life and realize that *things* just aren't cutting it. They just can't give us the protection from life that we had hoped. We are presented with the idea that Jesus Christ can be that protection for us and many of us buy into that. But what then? Is that it? Is that the end to the bulletproof life? Ticket paid and back to business as usual? No, actually it's just the beginning.

What we do will never save us. Remember, it can't. We are incapable. But what we do and how we do it does matter. Just like good tactics matter. It matters to God, it matters to us and it matters to the people around us.

It matters to God

In the same way that it would matter to a cop who stopped you, wrote your ticket and then paid it for you, it matters to God how we drive after that. To roar off again, spitting dust and rocks all over his police cruiser would be a complete abuse of the undeserved gift that he just gave you. And that's why it matters to God. He paid your ticket and even died to do it. Shouldn't there be a better way to respond to that? What we do in response to the grace that God has given to us is proof of our indebtedness and it speaks louder than our words ever could. What we do sends a message back to God that says, "Hey God, I haven't forgot what you've done for me. And I know I that I can't pay you back for that but I just want to show you how much I appreciate it."

Does it mean that we're going to do that perfectly? No. But God isn't expecting us to do it perfectly. He simply expects a natural cause and effect to take place in the relationship that we have with him. God caused us to be innocent; the natural effect is our thanks, both in our words and our actions.

It matters to us

We'll discuss how each specific tactic matters to us more in the chapters to follow, but they're a better way to respond to God's grace. These simple tactics bring us closer to God and work together to enhance his protection, just like a cop's tactics enhance his bulletproof vest's protection. When you hop in your car and pull the seatbelt across your chest, you don't drive off like a complete idiot just because you're wearing a seatbelt. You still drive with care and caution. You don't intentionally put your protection to the test.

Sure, you'll inevitably make mistakes as you go. But that's what the seatbelt is for; to save you when you can't save yourself. But there are plenty of opportunities for us to stay out of harms way that are totally and completely up to us; like driving at a safe speed, paying attention to the road and not becoming a rage on wheels. We have control over those things and the truth is that life is just better when we do them.

It matters to others

What we do after we become right with God matters to others too. Maybe in a way, it matters the most. Because what we do after we chose God isn't only a reflection of ourselves. When we start this new life with God, we become a reflection of God to the people around us. And you may be the only person they ever have a chance to see or know God through. And when you view it like that, what we do definitely begins to matter.

"Hey, I went to church yesterday." My teammate was being honest. He did go to church this Easter but his honesty was overshadowed by the sarcasm.

"Oh yeah, how was it?" I asked.

"It was alright."

"You going back?" asking but knowing the answer.

"Nah, too many hypocrites."

All over the world, people find the bulletproof life. They find a better way to live, enabled not by what they do or have, but by what Jesus Christ did for them. Many of those people dress up, go to church and worship God. But then come Monday morning, they fail at worshipping God in a tangible way. They might *talk about* Jesus Christ but they fail at *acting like* Jesus Christ to the world. That's why I think so many people view Christians as hypocrites. It's not so much that we stumble through it while trying to do it, because really, I think they could handle that. I think it's because, collectively, we just talk too much and act to little.

Author Brennan Manning was asked how it was possible that he became an alcoholic *after* accepting God's gift of grace and choosing to follow him. His response was not an excuse. It was a real life answer to real life bullets. He replied that it was possible because despite his new found life, God didn't turn him into an angel.[5] Life still hit Brennan like it hits everyone. And that pain led him to make some wrong choices.

Jesus Christ didn't make me an angel either. Just ask the cops I work with. But he did change everything about me. He changed my standing with God and how he sees me. He changed how I see myself. He changed how I see the world and the people in it. He changed my life in a way that I never could have changed on my own. He changed my heart and even though I still make wrong choices, my soul doesn't *want* to do them anymore. He changed my desires. I don't run around like some wanna-be-rock-star anymore or trust in *things* to save me. He changed the way I respond when I fall flat on my face. He changed the way I *want to* respond to people. Sure, I still fail. Sure, I still lose my temper, struggle with the way I talk and often fail miserably at showing the people I work with what God has done in me. But does that make me a hypocrite? Or just a bumbling Christian?

Remember those old, silent, black and white films with the cops running around in every direction and clutching their hats in their attempt to catch the bad guys? Those Keystone Cops, as they were referred, wore those full length black jackets, the tall rounded hats like the British police wear and carried those old school Billy clubs. The plot was always the same; the crooks broke the law and inevitably, a group of incompetent, bumbling cops showed up completely uncertain of what to do and making mistakes in everything they did do. The comedic scenes of them chasing the crooks around in silly, idiotic, bumbling fashion far outweighed any deficiencies in the stories plot. I can't even remember if they ever caught their man. I can't imagine they did. I was too enthralled in the silliness of their endeavor.

Hypocrites aren't people who always *do* what they believe. If that were the case, we'd all be considered hypocrites. Hypocrites are people who *pretend to be good* when in fact, they really aren't. And no doubt there are hypocrites in this world. It's just that the hypocrites that call themselves "Christians" have no understanding of their own sinful condition. They're people that fail to recognize that the need for God's grace is an everyday necessity and not just a one time event. They're most often the people pointing fingers, looking down on those *they deem* as "morally unjust" and shoving signs in people's faces. They don't care about people. They care about showing the world how good they are, when in fact it's painfully obvious they really aren't. And get this; those "Christians" may call themselves that but they're not following God the way that he intended.

But I think most people that truly choose to follow God are just a bunch of people who don't always do what they believe. They're Keystone Christians, with old habits that sometimes die hard and they're just bumbling their way through a tough life. Just like Brennan, just like me and just like you I imagine. God didn't *make me perfect* when I let him pay my ticket; he just began *viewing me* that way. What I am is an imperfect, bumbling, failing Christian trying to follow the guy that paid my ticket one day at a time. I'm not proud of that, that's just what I am. And that bothered me for a long time. I finally told God that I was sorry for that. I was sorry for being such a poor reflection of him and less than what I should be considering all that he has done for me. His response? Not a slap on the wrist followed by, "You hypocrite!" His response was the same as when he pulled me over. His response was amazing grace.

It wasn't this gushy idea of Jesus' arms wrapped around me and some soft, gentle, shepherd voice saying, "Its okay, I forgive you. Now, just stop screwing up." It was a reassuring feeling from God telling me, "You're going to bumble along. I'm not finished with you yet. But relax; you're no longer a criminal anymore." I had to process that. Maybe I am a bumbling Christian. All I know is that I'm not what I used to be and that gives me hope for tomorrow. This whole new life with God is not a one time event but a journey down a tough road filled with bumps, holes and every other obstacle that we can imagine. Is God concerned that we're bumbling Keystone Christians? I don't think so. I think he loves the fact that once we were criminals and now we aren't; that once we owed a debt that we could never repay and now we're living debt free; that once we were on the wrong side of the tracks of life and now we aren't. And that makes all the difference.

But make no mistake about it. Understanding this principle isn't a license for us to drive our lives any way we want to. God desires that we pursue a life that emulates the life of Christ. And that's important. It's important to God. It's important to us. And it's important to others. But what we can do is let go of the pressure of failing as we follow after God. In fact, our continued mistakes are a good reminder that we need just as much of God's grace in our everyday lives as everyone else. It also helps to keep us humble, dependent and so much more able to judge less and care more.

I don't know. Maybe the world does want to see perfect Christians. All I know is that I'll never be one and that if I would just shut up a lot more often and act like one a little more often; I would reflect Jesus Christ in a better way.

There is a better way to be bulletproof. They're called tactics. And the five that are listed here are not inclusive by any means. They're merely based on the principles of the five most basic police tactics. In fact, they're just a practical guide to get you started as you learn to follow after God on your own. Because there's no doubt that as you follow him, he'll begin to reveal himself to you in more ways than just what's listed here. Just remember this: doing them doesn't make you spiritually bulletproof. Only Jesus Christ can do that for you. And if you don't do them, God isn't going to yank his offer back. They're simply a better way to live your new found bulletproof life.

Drive safe.

———————————

* Johnny Cash was bulletproof (see *Cash* and *Man in Black*). John was only a boy when life first slammed into him when his older brother Jack died. Carrying that pain around, he began to slam into everyone around him. John eventually came back to God as a better way to live life and then lived it imperfectly, understanding the need to continually rely on God's grace until the day he died. We should be so fortunate.

** "Naked man with an axe," was Umberto's line when someone would inevitably ask him a stupid question like, "What's going on, officer?" His response, "Go back in your house; we're looking for a naked man with an axe."

8

TACTIC #1: COVER
Angel's wings

The art of war teaches us to rely not on the likelihood of the enemy's not coming, but on our own readiness to receive him; not on the chance of his not attacking, but rather on the fact that we have made our position unassailable.

-Sun Tzu*

When I was involved in my police shooting, the thing that I was most lacking was cover. Cover is anything that will stop incoming fire and is therefore considered the most important tactic there is. A bulletproof vest is considered portable cover but I wasn't wearing mine. Fixed cover items are such things as concrete walls, large trees and engine blocks of cars. But I didn't have those either. I was subjected to the best cover I had available, the back end of my car. But had my attacker fired on me, those bullets would have ripped through that car's thin sheet metal like a hot knife through butter. Don't get me wrong, I was thankful for what protection I had, however incapable it might have proved to be. I just knew that I was in a very bad tactical situation.

That's why the saying about tactical cover is, "Find cover and look for better cover."

On the street, during a violent attack, you should take cover immediately, no matter how poor it may be, while always looking for something better. The idea is that until you get to the place where you are totally and completely protected, you shouldn't stop looking for better cover. And since you'll probably never find the perfect cover on the street, never stop looking.

Some time later, in a post-incident interview, I had an imaginative flashback of the shooting scene. While at the time everything happened in fast forward, my flashback of that day was happening in slow motion. I was viewing it on the screen in my mind like *The Matrix* where Neo leans back in slow motion and dodges the incoming bullet.

Rather than seeing everything through my own eyes though, I was looking at myself from above, like some out of body experience. I saw myself standing there, reaching into my waistband and drawing my gun. As I punched my weapon forward and extended it towards my armed assailant, I saw an angel standing behind me. He spread his wings out, nearly ten feet wide in each direction and then wrapped them around me. I noticed that my arm was still extended out from between his wings, as if to say that he wasn't about to stop me from trying to kill the suspect, just that he was simply there to be my tactical cover. It was at that moment, in that weird visualization, that I fully understood the gravity of God's protection over me that day.

But as soon as I saw that incredible, angelic bulletproof protection, the picture in my mind rotated a hundred-and-eighty degrees. Now, I was looking at the suspect just as I saw him that night in a dark and filthy alley. His posture was forward, his face filled with hate, his arm extended in the same fashion as mine and his hand holding the pistol that could have killed me. But one thing was very different.

Angel wings had enveloped him as well. And as much as I understood God's protection over me that night, I understood that God was not about to let him die that night either.

Freeze that frame. The scene is a dark, dirty alley. Three story brick walls have a cop and crook hemmed in within fifteen feet of each other with guns drawn, ready to kill each other. The outcome should have been anything other than what it was. Someone, maybe even both of us, should have been seriously injured or killed that night. But someone was there protecting us. Both of us. God's hand of protection was there and not only on the cop.

As much as God saved me physically that night, he also saved me mentally and emotionally by not having to take another human life. I have always said that I could kill another human being if I had to but I hoped that I never had to. And God saved me from that too. But God also saved this guy from all those same things as well. It caused me to understand just a fraction of the amount of love that God must have and I wondered if my assailant would someday realize it too.

The crux of this new found bulletproof life is that God is our protection. Jesus did what we could not do for ourselves. He paid our ticket, made us right with God and therefore made us spiritually bulletproof for eternity. And that's the point. So before we go running around trying to, "Find cover and look for better cover" we just need to stand still behind the true cover that we already possess. This trust, that God has protected us from spiritual death once and for all, has to begin to permeate every other aspect of our lives. That's the on-going faith part of the bulletproof life. You trusted him once with your life, you can trust him again and again and again. Cover. It's the most important tactic there is. And when you stop, stand still and rest, you allow the God who is able, to protect you.

Two years after my shooting, a call came out for a bank robbery in progress. The bank personnel stated that the guy was armed. As we were flying to the call with lights flashing and sirens blaring, the dispatcher gave us an update that civilians were chasing the suspect on foot. I knew there was a good chance we would get there in time to chase him too and the possibility that I might end up in another shooting situation was growing higher by the second. Just prior to arriving, the civilians lost the suspect as he ran through the houses just north of the bank. Jimmy and I split up to set the perimeter and I found myself in another alley. I prepared myself for what I might have to encounter and took cover behind the corner of a garage.

I thought back two years earlier, into that other alley when I wasn't bulletproof. But this time was different. This time I was wearing body armor. This time I was behind cover. This time I was bulletproof. And that made all the difference in the world. I wasn't disabled by fear and panic, knowing that I might be shot within those next few luminous minutes. I was calm and ready to kill, if necessary. Mentally, I was being still behind the protection that I possessed and I had perfect peace about it.

The short story is that the suspect was contained within a two square block area. But before the K-9 units could arrive to safely search for the suspect, he broke into a house, robbed the owner of his wallet and keys and fled in the victim's car. A car chase ensued; he crashed, ran and was caught by my buddy…who ran him over with his police car.

God doesn't promise us that life will work out the way we think it should. God promises us that if we are on his side, we have his eternal, spiritual protection. He promises us that his protection can give us peace that the world will never stop searching for and will never find. So know this, and embrace it; the most important thing you will ever do in response to God's grace is to just stand still and let God be

God. In ways we can never imagine, the wings of God will surround you and you will find peace. So no matter what circumstance or situation you find yourself in, stop searching for better cover and just be still. You have already made your position, your life's final destination, unassailable.

---

* Sun Tzu is said to have penned, *The Art of War*. Believed to have been written somewhere between 722-221 BC, it has long been considered a masterpiece on military strategy and philosophy.

9

TACTIC #2: DISTANCE
Rumble in the Rockies

*We are not retreating; we are advancing
in another direction.*

-Douglas MacArthur

I'm sitting at my desk, leaning back, looking at the best 8"x10" photo of myself, ever. Living like I was a rock star had resulted in my fifteen minutes of shame. But the night this photo was taken, was my fifteen minutes of fame.

The year was 2003. The police boxing league had put together another boxing event. These, "smokers" as they were referred, occurred several times a year between members of our department and other departments across the nation and around the world. What drew me to this one was that it was a fund raiser and tribute to the victims of 9/11. And that meant we would be boxing the firefighters of New York City.

Even though I'd never officially boxed, I was pretty confident when I signed up. For one, I'd seen every *Rocky* movie there was and that alone seemed like a good start. And secondly, I had a bit of unofficial boxing experience from my old college days. When the Indiana boredom became too much to bear, a bunch of us would clear a room, pile in and watch as two guys commenced to punching each other into oblivion. And in all of my informal slug fests, I never lost. I even pounded those guys pretty good, nearly knocking two of them out. Yes, those were the glory days. The only problem was that I hadn't fought like that in nearly thirteen years.

The day prior to the fight came and the NYFD firefighters arrived. As each of us stepped on to the scale to weigh in, I saw my opponent for the first time. I sized him up and down and it was obvious that he was more than capable of handling himself in the ring. I pushed myself to focus on my game plan; get in close and then strike hard, strike fast and strike often. When I had boxed, I was never much of a boxer. I didn't dance around or move well. I just got in close and delivered the power, Mike Tyson style. And while that style had worked for me back in the Indiana cornfields, I just hoped it would work for me one more time.

Fight night

Fight night arrived and I was listed fifth on the fight card, which was fine with me. The butterflies were already swirling around in my stomach and I wanted as much time as possible to work them out. That's the big difference between fighting in the ring and fighting on the street. On the street, it just happens and you deal with it. But boxing was different. There was too much time to think about it and I didn't like that so much. But before I knew it, one fight had been scratched, another ended in a first round TKO and I was up, even though I didn't feel ready for it.

The event center was packed and people were cheering loudly. I made my way down the aisle, stepped onto the edge of the canvas and slid through the ropes into the ring. Suddenly, I couldn't see anything past the ropes. Just darkness. My whole world had shrunk down to the size of a small room. One that contained another man who was about to try to beat my brains in. What I was experiencing was tunnel vision, a form of compensation the body goes through in a stressful, hostile situation. It happens all the time on the street and I took a deep breath and relaxed when I recognized it. As I looked across the ring, I sized him up and down again. I knew the NYFD had a great boxing program but when I saw him decked out, wearing those professional high laced boxing shoes, I wondered what I had gotten myself into.

Because it was a 9/11 tribute, Michael Buffer was there announcing the fights. Michael's the guy who's announced some of the biggest professional boxer's names with his infamous bout opening phrase, "Let's get ready..." Sorry, can't finish it. Copyright. But you get the point. Anyways, it was a great experience. Not only to see him in person but to hear him announce my name accompanied by his infamous phrase.

"Ding, ding!"

The bell rang, the nerves wore off and the adrenaline kicked in. Now it was everything like the street. *Don't think, just rumble.*

Having watched other first time boxers fight, I knew they often came out swinging wildly and exhausted themselves in the first round. I was determined to not make that mistake and it didn't appear that he was going to either. We both came out snapping a few jabs, feeling each other out and fighting like pro boxers. But all of that quickly went out the window. He started unleashing haymakers and I realized he wasn't as polished a fighter as I had thought. Unfortunately, I got caught up in the moment and responded similarly. I guess I was no Rocky Balboa either. But I quickly recognized my mistake and tied up with him to settle myself down.

When the referee broke us apart, I was a little more at ease. I knew his wild punches were going to come again but this time I was just going to wait them out. *Don't dance, don't move. Just do what you do*, I thought. *Get in close and deliver the power.*

And I was right. He immediately went back to putting on the pressure, throwing a lot of punches but not landing anything that was bothersome. I relaxed and allowed him to push me back against the ropes and step straight into my danger zone. Then I delivered.

At thirty two seconds into the first round, I caught him with a right hook to his chin. A perfect punch. "Right on the button," as they say. His feet remained planted but the force of my glove against his face twisted his entire torso down and straight to the ground. His body lay there on the canvas, like a crumpled heap of human flesh. It was the same heap that I had been accustomed to seeing victims and suspects laying in on the street so many times. I'd even hit him so hard that his protective head gear had twisted on his head and concealed half of his face. I took a step forward and hovered above him. At that point, I was eagerly anticipating his rebuttal, ready to deliver more of that power should he rise from the ashes. But he never did.

That's the scene that was captured on film and the photo I'm looking at as I recount that day and write these words. Talk about feeling bulletproof. But the best part of that photo isn't me hovering over him inside the ropes. The best part is the ringside crowd's reaction, revealing their literal, jaw-dropping stunned faces.

More than five years later, I still get cops asking me if I was the guy who knocked out that New York firefighter. And I must sadly confess that my pride is often just as arrogant about it now as it was then. But it was actually pretty scary. I thought he might have been seriously hurt. He didn't get up for what seemed like an eternity.

Maximize and minimize

There's a reason they put men into a small ring. It's because there, in that close proximity, they are forced to engage each other. There is no safe distance. They are close and it's dangerous. But on the street, in real life force situations, the best way to win is to keep a safe distance from potential threats, engage only when necessary and when things are in your favor. That's the best case scenario. And quite frankly, we should probably do that a lot more often. Because once you get in close, it's too late. You're in a situation where there is often no other option but to go "hands on" and begin fighting, sometimes for your life. And that's just not the best way to do things.

My police training put it this way, "Maximize and minimize." Maximize the distance from the threat and [therefore] minimize yourself as a target. It's the same way in our life with God. Distancing yourself from compromising, dangerous, sinful situations is a better way to live a bulletproof life.

Can you have lunch with a female co-worker and not be sinning? Sure. But you've just placed yourself inside what we would call, "the outer perimeter." Once you enter that safety zone your ability to be harmed, or to harm others, has just been raised.

Maybe she makes you feel good about yourself and maybe she pays attention to you and maybe she gives you what you haven't been getting from your wife. It all may "feel good" and seem innocent enough, so you step closer to the threat and flirt with her. Before you know it, you've taken enough steps that you find yourself inside, "the inner perimeter." The inner perimeter is the area that is regarded as dangerously close to the action. At that point, the ice you're standing on is thin and you could go under with the slightest error. Now your options of not literally going "hands on" with her is decreasing exponentially. And just because everything "feels good" doesn't mean that it is. Your ability to avoid sin has now become extremely difficult.

God warns us not to put ourselves in precarious, dangerous situations. Not because he doesn't want us to have any fun or enjoy life but because he knows our weaknesses and wants us to have the best life possible. Infidelity, disease, an unwanted pregnancy, guilt, divorce, alimony, child support. Those aren't the things God intended when he created sex. And they're definitely not what we think of when we imagine the best life possible.

Not surprisingly, God's got a few good ideas about a lot of things. They're written all throughout his letter to us, called the Bible. They're ideas that will keep us safe from harm, ideas that will keep us from hurting others and ideas that offer us a better way to live life, if we're willing to give them a try.

Can you walk through the valley of the shadow of death because Jesus Christ has made you spiritually bulletproof? Absolutely. That's the whole point. Just don't take the road through that valley intentionally. There's a better way to respond to being bulletproof and choosing which direction to go is a part of it.

10

TACTIC #3: RESTRAINT
Posse up

Summon me, then; I will be the posse comitatus;
I will take them to jail.

-Samuel Chase

Early summer

It was about six o'clock on the morning. A bunch of us were about to go off duty in the next hour and were ending our shift the way we always did. Over breakfast. No, it was not a donut shop. It was a real live sit down restaurant. That served donuts.*

The dispatcher interrupted my breakfast, "221?"

I took another sip of my hot coffee before answering, "221."

"221, on a domestic at 4751 Compton Street. Contact a female who states that her husband hit her and is now gone."

"221, clear."

"Car to cover 221 on a domestic at 4751 Compton Street?"

I was still a boot but I had been on the job long enough to know that no one wanted to get up from breakfast and cover a domestic assault with less than an hour to go, especially when the suspect was already gone.

"Hey Gentry, I'll cover you. Just give me a minute."

"Nah, I got it Joe. But thanks."

I keyed my radio and told dispatch, "221, I'll advise on cover." Tactical mistake #1- Not accepting backup when backup is available.

As I made the drive across the district, the sun was beginning to rise and it was already warming up. I was ready to go home, cover the bedroom windows and go to bed. But I knew that I had to wake myself up and put my head in The Game for one last call.

"221, code six."

I pulled onto the block and parked a few houses away. I wasn't about to pull up right out front like I was a secretary there to take a report. I was a tactical cop and I was going to act like one whether the suspect was there or not. Anyways, who knows? Maybe he had come back to knock her around some more in the amount of time it took me to finish my coffee and get there.

It was quiet. Besides the evidence of the paperboy, it seemed like no one had come out this early yet. But I knew that someone had.

I knocked on the door and contacted a Hispanic female in her early thirties. She was jostling a baby in one arm and wiping tears from her eyes with the other. Her right eye already showed signs of trauma.

With no proper introduction, she let me in and I asked her what had happened. That's life in the hood. People want you to be kind and polite but they know who you are, so skip the generalities and get to the point.

Through her tears she said, "We were arguing and he tried to grab the baby. I yelled at him and he punched me."

Beyond all the personal information, that was all I needed. Before the state passed laws forcing us to make arrests for domestic violence, it was discretionary, based on the facts. Just the facts. And usually the facts were that even though we knew some jerk just hauled off on his wife or girlfriend, if she didn't say it and agree to prosecute him, not much was done. That's just the way it was. But this woman not only said it, she wanted him arrested. I love women with guts. At this point, it was obvious that I would be doing overtime. My mind settled it with my tired body and I prepared to suck it up.

"What's your husband's name?"

"There he is, right there." She pointed out the window and I saw a guy pulling up in a primer gray Olds Cutlass.

I stepped outside onto the porch and said, 'Hey, I need to talk to you."

I don't remember exactly what he said but it included the F-word, a middle finger and "Pig" as he sped off.

I stood there watching him as he took the corner too fast and could hear his wheels screeching until he was completely out of sight. I figured there was absolutely no reason to tell the dispatcher that he came back because he was already gone. Besides, the Detail One boys were now on their way home and the day shift cops were most likely getting ready to start their day the same way that ours ended. I wasn't about to have other cops playing cat and mouse over a simple domestic at 0700 hours. *Besides, what's the likelihood he'll come back with the cops here?* Tactical mistake #2- Not starting backup.

I obtained all the information that I needed to put a warrant out for his arrest, advised her of some things she could do to protect herself, such as staying with a family member and getting a temporary restraining order and walked back to my car. Now, I had watched several slugs just hop in their cars and drive back to the safety and comfort of the station to finish the paperwork. But I didn't come on the job to be a slug. *I might as well park down the block while I write this up. Maybe the pig hating, wife beater will come back.*

Before I was even done writing the report, he pulled up in front of the house again. As mad as he was when he punched her the first time and as mad as he was when he drove up and saw the cops there, he was even madder now. I could see it in his eyes from a block away and it was obvious that he was going to take it out on her, again.

I keyed my radio, "221, Can I get a cover car code nine? The suspect just returned." Okay, I admit it. I screwed up. I should have let Joe cover me or asked for that cover car as soon as he had come back the first time.

"Car to cover 221 on a domestic at 4751 Compton Street?"

The fact that the dispatcher heard me was good enough for me. I wasn't waiting for someone to answer her or for them to get there. Who knew how long that would take? I pulled the gear selector down into drive and stomped on the gas. I had known full well that if he came back, I was going to contact him, with or without cover. You see, every cop has their own pet peeves. That's why some cops actually get mad at you when you're speeding. It's more than the fact that you're breaking the law; it's the unfortunate fact for you that it's one of his pet peeves. Every cop has them. Mine, is wife beaters. You hit a woman and so much as raise a finger to me, you're going see what being hit is all about. Tactical mistake #3- Not waiting for backup.

I pulled up, blocked his escape this time with the front end of my Crown Vic and jumped out. The anger in his eyes turned to fear. I walked up to his driver door and ordered him to get out. As he opened the car door, I could see a can of mace lying on the seat next to him. I wasn't sure who that was intended for but I wasn't going to wait and find out. I immediately grabbed his arm but he jerked away and shoved me. *Game on, boy.*

I tackled him and attempted to handcuff him. If fighting isn't hard enough, you should try handcuffing someone who doesn't want to be handcuffed. When he kept resisting and swinging wildly, like any good wife beater would, I pulled out my sap and commenced to bring him into submission. ** *Not as easy as a defenseless woman, huh?*

We tumbled from the middle of the street into the grass and I ended up on top of him. He was still unwilling to give up and the very fact that he was continuing to fight with the police was driving the stakes up. I had to be aware of retaining my own gun at this point. No way was some cowardly wife beater going to take my gun away and kill me with it. I began to rain down with the sap like a heavy storm but soon realized it wasn't producing the compliance that I wanted. I tossed it, reached for another tool on the old tool belt and unleashed a blast of mace towards his face. A mist of orange liquid began covering his face. He kept fighting, I kept macing. When he could no longer see or breathe, he gave up and I was able to cuff him without any more resistance. *See, you should've given up to begin with. But I appreciate that you didn't.* Tactical mistake #4- Trying to be John Wayne.

The battered woman had come out of the house and was now walking towards us. I yelled at her to stay back because I didn't know if she was mad at the fact that I just beat the guy up that had just beat her up. I realized that I was still jacked up on enough adrenaline to have tunnel vision. I couldn't see if she had a knife or any other potential weapon in her hand and didn't want to end my shift being stabbed in the back or cracked over the head with a frying pan. Don't laugh, that kind of thing happens.

I took a few deep breaths and with the suspect screaming in the background, asked the dispatcher for a sergeant and an ambulance.

Once they both calmed down, he started crying for her and she started crying for him. The fight was over and my rage had worn off. She wanted to attend to him by washing his face off and knowing how horrible that stuff is, I felt compassionate enough to let her. I just hoped that deep down there was an ounce of satisfaction in her that he got a dose of what he just gave out. I know I did.

My sergeant arrived to see the crying, beat up wife watering her crying husband's beat up, orange face with a garden hose. He just stood there, casually observing the moment and finally commented, "Love. Ain't it grande?"

Tactical restraint is not shortcutting your bulletproof protection by going in alone. And that being my biggest tactical restraint blunder to date, it was a good lesson early in my career that taught me there is a better way to respond. Utilize back up whenever back up is available. A spiritually bulletproof life is no different. So, if you want to live with God's enabling power in your life, there is a better way to do it. Posse up.

Three's not a crowd

How many cops does it take to solve a crime? I don't know they haven't showed up yet. -Anonymous

For the record, it takes at least three cops to solve a crime. The first cop shows up, investigates the crime, does the initial paperwork and captures the suspect; the second invariably stands around and watches without even offering to help and the third reminds the other two that its time to grab some donuts. No wonder they're never around when you need one, they're eating donuts in three's.

Just like the street, God never intended that we try to face life's obstacles all alone. I'm not telling you to go hold hands with some dude, join a club or to even go to church. I'm telling you what you already know to be true, that life is hard. I'm telling you that you don't have to navigate through that hard life all alone. I'm telling you that the bulletproof life is better in three's: you, God and someone to back you up. I'm telling you that if you can partner up with someone else that has chosen to follow God, it's just a better way to live.

I've had my share of trying to be John Wayne, both on the street and against life's struggles. And honestly, it's not that great. Don't get me wrong, a street fight is thrilling. But real life fights have a way of ending up in real bad ways and if I have my choice, I'd rather outnumber the bad guy every time. The same goes for real life events. I've faced some stuff that I tried to take on alone and it rocked my world every time.

Go in alone? Are you crazy? Fight fair? Says who? The guys on the street that we have to fight don't fight fair and life certainly isn't going to fight fair with you. So why try to take on life alone?

I can assure you that when life lands a good punch on your chin or connects with a bullet that seems to burn a hole through your chest, it's comforting, encouraging and powerful all at the same time to be able to confide in people that believe in the same God that you do. When I've admitted to those that I trust, "Man, life sucks right now," or "I don't know how to handle this," or "I screwed things up," I know that I'm not going to get a wrong answer. That answer may not be what I *want* to hear but I am assured it's what I *need* to hear. Sometimes that's just a sympathetic, "I'm sorry you're going through that," or an honest, "I don't know what to tell you," or the hardest one, "Yeah, you screwed up. You need to make that right." But whatever the answer is, I know that having someone to back me up in this life is just as important as having it on the street.

Sure you can live a bulletproof life all alone. But God never intended for it to be that way. He intended for it to be better than that. He intended that we live tactically bulletproof by partnering up and stacking life in our favor when life's bullets are coming at us. One way is a better way. And the faster you can partner up, the faster you won't have to square off with life all by yourself.

----

* Donut jokes? Come on. They don't offend me; they're just old. My reply is always the same, "Do I look like I eat donuts? New breed. Whole wheat bagels. Now get lost."

** A blackjack or "sap" is a flat piece of leather loaded with a heavy piece of lead in one end. It is designed to strike soft tissue and increase pain in order to gain compliance. After the fight with the wife beater, I realized that the stitching on the end of the sap had come apart and the lead had flown out. I was basically spanking this guy like my dad had done to me with his old leather belt. No wonder it wasn't working on him, it hadn't work on me either.

11

TACTIC #4: SURPISE
"Knock, knock."

Attack him where he is unprepared,
appear where you are not expected.

-Sun Tzu

Nothing is more exhilarating for me on the force than kicking down doors. Maybe it's because I watched so many TV cops do it and quite frankly, it just looked cool. Maybe it's because of the fact, that even in the best of circumstances, you really have no idea who or what is waiting for you on the other side of that door. Maybe it's because it's the epitome of police power, pushing the limit of American's Forth Amendment rights to be secure against unreasonable search and seizure. Or maybe, it's just because it's such a display of physical power. Nothing says, "Knock, knock. It's the police, can we come in?" like the sole of my Magnum combat boot hitting a door with full force.

While working Detail One, I'd received a domestic violence call. Dispatch advised that a male suspect was threatening a female with a kitchen knife. Umberto got the call to cover me and he arrived at the run-down, two-story apartment building just as I was pulling up. With the hot summer air and only a few tenants being able to afford air conditioning, we could hear a woman's screams through a first floor open window.

"Looks like this one, 'eh Berto?"

"Yeah, looks like."

We weren't being sarcastic. In most neighborhoods, you could run towards the sound of a woman's scream to rescue her. But on the wild side, in the inner-city, that wasn't always the case. Sometimes your ear had to wade through the sounds of a lot of people who were screaming, fighting and otherwise carrying on.

As we continued to approach the building through the darkness, I noticed the window blinds were pulled open. Because the lights were on inside and the darkness outside, we were able to creep up to the window without being seen. I cautiously peeked above the window sill and saw a man and woman arguing. In his right hand was a twelve inch kitchen knife. I drew my gun and watched for a second, waiting to see how this was going to develop and to decide the best way to engage him.

The woman was standing to my right, about two feet away, with her back to me. The suspect was standing in the doorway, about ten feet away and facing me. The knife was dangling loosely in his hand down along side of his leg. He wasn't wielding it in a threatening way but I knew that could change at any second. All I knew was that if he chose to use it, it was long enough to do some serious damage. Still unnoticed, I raised my pistol sights up over the window sill and leveled them on his chest. *If you're ever going to be involved in a shooting, this is the one you want.*

I was an expert marksman and I was completely calm. I had a clear shot, right through the glass window, should I need to take it. My finger rested safely along the weapon's frame just above the trigger as I thought through all four firearm rules.

1) *Treat all weapons as if they were loaded.* Mine was locked, cocked and ready to roll.
2) *Never let the muzzle of your weapon point at anything you aren't willing to destroy.* If he was willing to stab her, I was willing to destroy him.
3) *Never put your finger on the trigger until you are prepared to shoot.* My index finger was still safely along the frame. If he raised the knife or took a step closer, my finger was ready to drop onto the trigger and take care of business.
4) *Always be aware of your target and beyond.* I was aware of the apartment behind them. If I didn't land the shot, there was a good chance that my bullet would go through the walls and into some innocent person's living room.

Unlike my shooting, this time I was armed with my full-size duty weapon. With eighteen rounds of 9mm in the holding pattern, all they were waiting for was permission to takeoff. *Is he going to choose life or death?* That decision depended only on what he did next and he didn't even realize it.

As fast as it could have escalated, it de-escalated. The suspect tossed the knife on the bed, turned around and walked into the living room. But hell hath no fury like a woman scorned and she marched right behind him, presumably to get the last word in. That's when I knew this thing could easily go from zero to sixty again, like a Brahma bull out of the shoot.* Berto and I followed along outside of the apartment, peeping through the windows as we went, keeping tabs on the situation. As we accessed the building and finally stood alongside the suspect's front door, we could still hear them arguing. Berto and I quickly made the decision to maintain our silence and tactically surprise him by kicking in the door.

Just as I was about to rear back and kick the door in, Berto whispered, "Let's both kick it."**

"Sounds good," I whispered back.

I'd never done that before but thought, *If kicking in doors is a thrill, two cops kicking it has to be twice the thrill.* Hey, it sounded logical at the time.

Berto started counting quietly, "One."

I started thinking about Mel Gibson and Danny Glover in Lethal Weapon 2 when Sgt. Murtaugh is sitting on a booby trapped toilet. *Is it one, two, three and kick? Or one, two, and kick on three?* Suddenly, logic had become way too complicated. But before I could stop him for some clarification, Berto had already counted off, "Two" and "Three" came too fast.

"Three!"

We both planted with our left foot and kicked with our right. Tactical lesson learned: Don't do what you don't train to do. I yelled out in pain, "Ah! You just kicked me in the ankle!"

My first reaction was to punch Berto in retaliation for his poorly placed door knock but I was too enthralled with what I saw. The door didn't fly open as usual. It exploded at all three hinges and fell flat into the middle of the living room like a medieval draw bridge. The surprised couple stood there wide eyed and jaw dropped, looking at us as we looked at them, until we finally announced our presence. "Knock, knock."

A surprising letter

Armies expect to fight when they're prepared, not to be attacked when they aren't. Bullies expect the people they prey on to back down, not to take a step forward and stand up to them. And crooks expect civilized cops to knock, not to kick their doors down like barbaric thugs.

The truth is that the world expects certain things. But you have the ability to surprise the world. When you make a mistake, make it right. When someone is in need, provide. When the world does you wrong, hold no grudge. Does it make sense? Absolutely not. But then again, it doesn't make sense that Jesus Christ paid your ticket either. There is a better way to live the bulletproof life and to effectively share it with the world around you. And surprising them, in your own unique way, is a better way.

Timothy Steinberg is a convicted murderer. He not only killed several men but one of them was a Federal Bureau of Prisons correctional officer. Just like I was. He stabbed him over 38 times. And he's been in solitary confinement ever since. Nearly twenty-five years. Today I wrote him a letter.

Tim,

Can I call you that? Timothy seems so formal and the moniker, Terrible Timmy, well...I just don't think that's who you really are anymore. Anyways, I just finished reading an article about how you killed that hack. And about how you feel tortured by the Bureau by living in solitary confinement for so long. And about how the guards have treated you horribly because you killed one of their own. And how the death penalty would have served you just fine compared to having to live in solitary confinement for the past 25. And I just want to say, I'm sorry that you've had to endure that. I'm sorry that life has hit you like it has. But I also want you to know that I forgive you. And God forgives you. And I pray that Jesus Christ would not only widen the walls of your heart but the physical ones that torment you as well. And

Tim, I just want you to know one more thing. I was a BOP hack.

Officer G. T. Gentry
Federal Bureau of Prisons (ret.)

I don't know if Tim ever got that letter, if he even cared or if he'll ever respond. I just know that there is only one person in this world that it would even matter to him to hear those words. And that one person was an under-paid, jaded, prison hack.

God didn't call us to surprise those who treat us right. Everyone does that. He called us to surprise our enemies, because without him, that's not even possible. Does that mean it's easy? No way. It may be one of the hardest tactics to ever develop. In fact, if you're anything like me, I can assure you that you will fail at it time and again. But in those moments you do succeed, you allow God to appear in someone else's life at a place they never expected for him to appear. And that is a surprise worth giving.

---

* "This bull will take you 0-60 in about two seconds." That was my Lieutenant's warning just before I rode a Brahma bull. I did it once. And I don't know if the bull hit 60 mph but two seconds is about all I lasted. Thankfully, that was the end to my bull riding career.

** Berto's door kicking days were short. He earned the, "Pink Slipper Award" for softly "punting" another door numerous times in an effort to get it open. Eventually the fire department arrived and opened it for him.

12

TACTIC #5: INVISIBLE DEPLOYMENT
The Trojan horse

O divine art of subtlety and secrecy!
Through you we learn to be invisible.

-Sun Tzu

Let me backup for a minute. Umberto is three generations deep on the force. He's tall and gangly but a good looking guy who's both crazier and funnier than anyone I've ever met on the job. Luckily for that sailor mouth of his, it came complete with a silver spoon in it. With which he did not disappoint Internal Affairs or the ladies. Which by the way, is how he married up. Now, it's not hard for a cop to marry up. We're not the most social or affluent bunch. But Berto married way up; established certified, MD issue.

Berto's a genuine guy's guy. He's tough as nails; just ask him, he'll tell you. But he's not so hard that he snubs anyone. He'll tell you to suck it up when something needs sucking up but he'll also be there for you at the drop of a hat when you need it. I've missed working with him ever since he moved from the rank and file to an illustrious detective position.* And Berto, you actually do look better in a suit than a uniform.

But one night we got Berto good.

We were working Detail One and were already hours into our shift. It was nearly 0200 hours. It was summer and still nearly eighty degrees out. The calls for service had slowed down to zero. The radio had been silent for over an hour. There wasn't a drug addict, gang member or prostitute creeping around anywhere. It was as if God said, "Okay criminals, its time to go to bed," and they did. And that made the protectors of the city bored. Berto was off that night and his house was in the district. It was a perfect setup.

I don't remember who actually came up with the idea but it's still a classic and yet to be outdone.

We gathered everyone who was up for it, dropped the game plan and broke the huddle. Assignment: Spread out through the district and comb the alleys and dumpsters for furniture. We were about to fully furnish Berto's front yard with a complete living room set.

And that's exactly what we did as we kept our ear to the radio. Thankfully, other officers weren't interested in dumpster diving were willing to take those calls had they come up. But the city assisted us anyways and the radio remained silent.

I don't know how many alleys it took but I finally found a reclining chair and loaded it up. As I pulled up to the house to unload it, Jimmy pulled up behind me with an old TV set. We giggled quietly like two school girls as we placed them on the curb in front of Berto's house and jumped back in our cars to go find more. I wasn't gone long before I had to call him.

"Jimmy, come over to the 2600 block of Holmes, in the alley. I just found a full size couch." Without a word, the phone was silent and there he was.

"Gees, you scared me. What are you, some kind of superhero?"

"I was just around the corner. Sweet couch. 70's fabric. Nice touch."

We lifted the couch into my trunk and I sped off towards Berto's house. I wasn't sure if that thing was going to hold back there and kept checking my rearview mirror. Even though the streets were completely barren, the last thing I wanted to tell my sergeant was that a couch fell out of the trunk of my police car, into the middle of the road, in the middle of the night and that someone had crashed into it. Explaining the, "Why was it there in the first place?" would have been another issue.

Luckily, the couch made it safely back to Berto's and Jimmy helped me unload it. The growing pile of furniture was evidence that the other cops were doing their jobs as well. There, dumped on the curb in front of Berto's house was a couch, chair, coffee table, electric fan, area rug and an end table.

"This is awesome," I quietly told Jimmy but this time we both started laughing hysterically.

The whole thing was working out better than we had hoped. Having everything we needed, we set out once more for the, "icing on the cake." Before long, everyone returned to the house for final assembly. I was one of the first to arrive and watched as police cars drove silently down the street with their lights off. One trunk was up. That was a good sign. Then, two cops unloaded an old, standing organ!

Alan rolled up and was smiling ear to ear. "I got it."

"You got it? Better than the organ? Well, let's see it."

"Not until everything else is set up."

We quickly laid everything out so that it was all facing the street. That way, the early bird neighbors, who would be wiping the sleep out of their eyes in a few hours, would see it just as if they were looking through Berto's front living room window.

"Well, what do you got?" I asked Alan with growing anticipation.

He went to his trunk, put on a pair of rubber gloves and walked back with a dead cat. "Who doesn't have a pet?"

And that's when everyone lost it. As I laughed, I cringed at the volume we were producing, hoping the neighbors or even Berto himself wouldn't hear us and wake up. But then again, what if they did? Who were they going to call? The police?

Alan placed the cat on the couch with its front legs and head draped over the arm of the chair so that it looked like it was taking a nap. We took some Polaroid photos for posterity and we all drove off laughing hysterically.

I met up with Jimmy a few blocks away at an empty parking lot.

"You know what would have blown this thing out of the water?" he asked.

"What's that?"

"If we could have got a bum to fall asleep on the couch!"

"Stop it! You're killing me." My face was starting to hurt I was laughing so hard.

When Ms. Berto woke up the next morning, she looked outside expecting to see a normal morning sunrise as it lit her front lawn. Instead, the good doctor saw what she thought she would never see. Her scream flooded the quiet morning air, "Berto!"

Looking at the picture in hand, I'm dreading the day of retaliation. The scorn of a woman, especially one with money, is a dangerous thing. But what makes me more nervous is that the scorn has been brewing now for over seven years. It's not going to be pretty, but until then Berto, we are king of the hill.

A better way to deploy

I could have used several cops vs. bad-guy stories to convey the idea of invisible deployment but I just love that story. Besides, talk about invisibly appearing, a whole living room invisibly appeared on Berto's front lawn.

The tactic of invisible deployment is to show up unseen. Its benefit is obvious. If they don't know you're there, it's less likely they can hurt you. Because believe me, if Berto knew we were there in his lawn that night, he would have hurt us. Severely. And while it may seem to be synonymous with the tactic of surprise, it's different and actually precedes the surprise. You can't be invisible after you surprise someone. It has to come first. Because isn't that how you surprise someone? You show up first, unnoticed and then jump out and yell, "Surprise!"

And that is what this book was designed to do. It was designed to invisibly deploy God's truth to people who might not have otherwise read a book about God. A Trojan horse of sorts. The only difference is that this device wasn't designed to destroy you like the city of Troy. It was designed to over-take you with God's love, mercy and grace and to give you life. And if you are offended by that ruse, I apologize to you. But think of the positive; at least you don't have a front yard full of old furniture.

If that tactic did work, then mission accomplished. Now you have a tool to invisibly deploy into someone else's life. Or better yet, invisibly deploy yourself into their life in your own way. Find ways to connect with them on a personal level, understand their situation and circumstances and invest yourself into their life. That's a far more effective way to share the bulletproof life than shoving a megaphone in their face, pointing fingers and shouting stuff they've heard a million times. That stuff will just make you look like a hypocrite. You want to share the bulletproof life you've got? Don't tell them. They've had enough of that. Show them. That's the whole reason that I wrote this book for Shane. He's heard enough talking. It was time to embrace the lost art of subtlety and secrecy and invisibly place myself into a position to show him that I not only care about the storms in his life but about his soul as well.

A preface to the Part Three

To stop here would be more than an injustice; it'd be just plain, poor police work. And if I were to stop here, I might as well stop chasing crooks down, grab a handful of donuts... and become a lieutenant. Because as a cop, I have a responsibility to do more than just accuse people of crimes. I have a responsibility to produce a certain amount of evidence to support that accusation. And since I just spent the last twelve chapters claiming that Jesus Christ not only changed my life but promising you that he can change yours, I darn well owe you some evidence to support that.

---

* "Illustrious detective position," is an oxymoron. There is no such thing.

13

CSI: THE EVIDENCE

The first thing we do is kill all the lawyers.

-Shakespeare

I was at the station finishing up my reports when the call came out. It was a rape in progress. I sat there for a second thinking if I should go or not. The location was half way across the district and I was about to go home for the night. Besides, I figured that either the suspect would be long gone by the time I got there or someone else had to be closer. I hesitated one more second before I leaped up and ran out the door. Jumping in my cruiser, I hit the lights and siren and raced down Marshall Avenue at over a hundred miles per hour. I told you. I can't drive fifty-five.

As I got closer, the dispatcher revised the information, "All cars, the suspect is a black male, wearing a white shirt and bleeding from the back. Apparently the homeowner stabbed him and he's now chasing the suspect on foot north from that location. Be advised that the suspect may also be armed with a knife."

My adrenaline started to flow like a busted dam. I was within twenty blocks from the assault now and I realized there just might be a chance at catching this guy.

Dispatch, "All cars on this sex assault, the homeowner is calling back now stating that he lost the suspect. Last seen eastbound at 22nd and Queen."

I was within blocks of that location. I made a left turn where the suspect was last seen, turned off my headlights and began slowly trolling through the neighborhood, looking and listening for anything out of the ordinary. I made another left and started down a residential street. Out of the corner of my eye, I caught a glimpse of something. I thought I saw someone or something on the other side of a parked car. My heart rate spiked. I stopped to check it out.

Before I could get out of my patrol car, a man jumped up and began running. It was dark but not so dark that I couldn't see that he was a black male, wearing a white t-shirt and bleeding from the upper left shoulder. I'm no detective but I had a pretty good clue that this was my guy. I began to chase after him on foot and noticed how dark it really was. The only available light was that from a few sparsely located street lights. I immediately knew that if I lost sight of him in that darkness, I was not only in much greater danger but even worse, he might get away. And I wasn't about to let that happen. I continued to chase him, through the houses and towards the alley.

I wasn't exactly sure where I was, it all happened so fast but I aired that I was in pursuit of the suspect from where he was last seen. Within seconds, I could hear the wail of sirens in the distance as cops began speeding towards me to help. And let me tell you, that's one of the most comforting sounds I've ever heard.

As I cut through the houses in pursuit, I lost sight of him. I didn't want to get ambushed and possibly stabbed, so I cautiously maneuvered my way around the next corner. Once

I safely accomplished that, I saw him again. He was running south down the middle of the alley and then jumped a fence into another backyard to the east. Fortunately, he got caught in the fence. As he was trying to free himself, I was able to quickly cover the lost ground and catch up to him. When he realized that I was right behind him, he turned around and looked me directly in the face.

There was a momentary pause but it seemed like an eternity. We were no farther than a few feet away from each other and the only thing separating us was a three-foot, chain link fence. It was a surreal moment that I'll remember my entire life. Our eyes were fixated for that split second but my peripheral vision caught a glimpse of something shiny in his right hand. With my gun pointed directly at his chest, I still couldn't look away from his face. The hate and fear in his eyes was compelling.

I finally yelled at him, "Drop the knife!"

"Go ahead and kill me," he responded with an eerily calm voice.

I didn't know it then but I think he really did want me to kill him. He knew what I didn't; that he was a habitual violent offender and this was going to put him down for a very long time. Just as I was about to pull the trigger and end this man's life, he broke free and started running again. I quickly holstered my pistol, jumped the fence and tackled him. Surprisingly, he offered less resistance than I would have imagined and I was able to quickly handcuff him. *At least the wife beater fought back.*

Once in custody, the victims were brought to the scene for a "show up." There, the victim and her boyfriend positively identified him as the man who had broke into their house, attempted to rape her at knifepoint and who told her that if she screamed, he would kill her baby. That brave woman had refused to be a victim. She fought him tooth and nail and just long enough for her boyfriend to come up from the basement, investigate her scream, stab her attacker in self defense and chase him down the street as he escaped.

If the glove don't fit, you must acquit

Months later, serial rapist and career criminal, Terrance Lee Williams was convicted of aggravated assault and attempted rape. He was sentenced to 144 years in prison. And do you know what caused those twelve jurors to so easily decide Williams' guilt and send him to prison where he belonged? Two things. The first was the three eyewitnesses who took the stand, raised their right hand and swore to tell the truth, the whole truth and nothing but the truth. And the second was the cold, hard facts.

The eyewitness testimonies were; one woman's painful account of how she was attacked, in fear for her life and nearly raped; one man's heroic account of how he fended off his girlfriend's attacker and then chased him from their home; and one cop's gritty account of how he nearly shot and killed the suspect just before taking him into custody.

The cold, hard facts of the case were; Williams' bloody shirt that he was wearing when arrested, his matching blood on the homeowner's kitchen knife and his fingerprints that were found strewn about the victim's home. Unfortunately for Terrance Lee Williams, all of those evidentiary gloves fit. How could the jury acquit?[*]

That's the importance of evidence, whether it's eyewitness testimony, the cold, hard facts or both. It has the power to take us from merely understanding to believing something enough to bet our whole life on.[**]

Take this for example, eventually I was no longer satisfied with understanding the protective capabilities of my bulletproof vest that the police academy had spoon fed me to believe. I wanted to believe it, with everything I had, but I also wanted proof that I could see and touch. I wanted to know for myself that my body armor would stop a bullet.

I wanted to know firsthand what my life was depending upon. So, I finally took an old bulletproof vest to the firing range, shot it, cut it open and examined it. And when the evidence proved to do what it claimed it could do, it changed everything.

And it's no different spiritually. That's the whole reason for these last few chapters. This is your opportunity to examine the proof that you can see and touch. This is your opportunity to know that God is willing to do all that he said he would do. This is your opportunity to know, firsthand, what your eternal, spiritual life is depending upon. So take this opportunity in these next few chapters to rip open, dissect and examine the evidence surrounding *A Bulletproof Life*. Then you will know what would cause that one British commander and so many others before him and since, to so confidently trust their *souls* to when they uttered those three little words..."But. If. Not!"

---

* Does anyone really believe that O.J. didn't do it? Come on. That case is a perfect example why we should take Shakespeare's advice and kill all the lawyers.

** If you're interested at the examination of evidence, I recommend you watch the movie, *12 Angry Men*. It's an old-school black and white movie starring Henry Fonda. It doesn't have the action or special effects of today's great cop movies but it does reveal the process of twelve men as they dissect numerous, "What if" questions and deliberate over the fate of a man charged with murder.

14

THE WHOLE TRUTH...

*I came here to tell you the truth, the good,
the bad and the ugly.*

-Oliver North

The only thing more damning to a person accused of a crime than an eyewitness is multiple, independent, non-collaborating eyewitnesses with no motive to provide us with anything but the truth, the whole truth and nothing but the truth. Such was the case in this most recent homicide trial...

A certain professor was accused of murdering a wealthy man named Mr. Body in the conservatory of his mansion with a candlestick. The problem was that the police weren't able to find a lick of hard, physical evidence. But what they were able to produce were several eyewitnesses. Five of them to be exact. Three women, one gentleman and a colonel.

Now the professor, being the scholar that he is, thought he had been meticulous in the execution of the crime. *The perfect crime,* he thought. Ah, but is there such a thing? Unbeknownst to the professor, three women happened to be talking and smoking on the grounds just outside the conservatory and saw the horror through the large open windows. The gentleman, who had just finished a game of pool in the billiard room, walked past the conservatory and witnessed the murder through the crack of the door that had been inadvertently left ajar. And the colonel, who had been snooping around Mr. Body's mansion, saw it all as he stopped in his tracks just before entering the conservatory through the secret passage from the lounge!

So suppose for a moment, each of our eyewitnesses did see the professor kill Mr. Body in the conservatory with the candlestick. And, for sake of an argument, let us assume that our five witnesses were all strangers, that they had not met the professor prior to the night in question and that they did not have an opportunity to collaborate their stories, as they had all been separated by the police immediately upon their arrival. Wouldn't that provide us with five, independent, non-collaborating witnesses with no motive to provide us with anything but the truth? And wouldn't that, even if we were absent any hard, physical evidence at the professor's trial, make for convincing proof of his guilt?

And that's what we have here; five, independent, non-collaborating witnesses, with no motive to provide us with anything but the truth. In fact, and as you will see, they don't try to paint their lives with shades of their own goodness. They tell us the truth; the good, the bad and the ugly. But they all have one thing in common. They all, independently and unanimously, point to Jesus Christ and testify that he's the one responsible for changing each of their lives.

Crossing over from death to life

I tell you the truth; whoever hears my word and believes him who sent me has eternal life and will not be condemned; he has crossed over from death to life. John 5:24 (NIV)

Although I accepted Christ's forgiveness when I was eleven years old, I didn't live for God much of my adult life. In fact, it was only by the grace of God that I even survived early adulthood. As I look back, now in my forties, I am amazed at what God brought me through. It's a testament of His love and continued care for us even when we may not be walking with Him in our daily lives. This is such a testimony.

My public service career started in 1990 with the U.S. Army as a Combat Medic. Within months of completing Basic Training, I received orders to ship out to the Gulf War. After arriving there, my unit was bivouacked in Saudi Arabia as we waited for the rest of our equipment to arrive. These thousand or so stationary troops made our location a target rich environment.

The first Scud Missile launched at our position was the most stressful incident I've ever lived through. And with each successive missile, the military P.A. would announce, "Scud launch, MOP level One." Those warnings were updated every few minutes, "Scud launch, ten minutes to impact... seven minutes to impact...four minutes to impact," and the terror of helplessly waiting for an in-coming missile, with nowhere to hide was horrifying. All I could do was pray.

Suddenly, a loud fiery bolt of light crossed the sky in front of me. It was followed by a brilliant flash and then, "BOOM!" I jumped and dove for cover. Fortunately, it wasn't a gas attack as we had been warned it might be. It was a Patriot Missile that had intercepted the Scud and saved us. That happened thirty two times. I find it interesting, looking back, how we go along life's path with no thought of God until you find yourself in a situation like this. Then it's, "Oh God save me!" But unknown to me at the time, God wasn't finished protecting me from more near misses...

I returned home from the Gulf War and continued my medical career as an EMT/Firefighter. For the next five years,

I not only began to face my own mortality more often but saw the death of others more often as well. The most difficult death, and one of the lowest times of my life, was the murder of my only brother. And while the pain of his death caused me to pray to God again, I still didn't consider living for Him. You might think that would have been enough to get my attention, but with shame I have to say, it didn't. Instead, I continued to live in my own world, not realizing all the while, that God was still there, refusing to leave my side.

Eventually, my life style took its toll on my marriage and I divorced, for a second time. I quit my job, put myself through the police academy and found a new home with the Sheriff's Department. I eventually remarried, had two incredible kids and became an SRT (Special Response and Tactics) team member.

On my daughters first birthday, our SRT team received a call-out on an armed and barricaded suspect. I kissed my wife and daughter goodbye and ran to my vehicle to respond. Little did I know that my wife was about to have a premonition that I would be shot in the head.

After arriving on scene, we briefed and prepared for entry. As we approached the house, I could see the suspect standing in the doorway holding a pistol. Following our commands, he dropped the gun, but then the fight was on. He eventually grabbed my arm and as I struggled to keep possession of my weapon, we stumbled into the residence. My pistol flipped out of my hand and landed on the coffee table. As I grabbed it, we both fell and crashed through the table causing the weapon to discharge. My wife's premonition was almost right. The round zipped past my head and lodged into the wall. I could barely see due to the muzzle flash, but thankfully it was enough to make the suspect surrender.

From what should have been another death sentence, God had spared me yet again. This time, He not only got my attention but I understood the message that He had a plan for my life. My wife and I joined a local church and I finally began a closer, personal walk with God.

I wish I could say that was the end and we lived happily ever after. A short time later, I began to have panic attacks. Up to this point, my fears of death had all been rational. My threats had all been real. But now I was having irrational fears of dying. No threats, just afraid. The attacks became so bad that I could no longer even go to work. I began to plead and pray to God to save me mentally and emotionally as He had spiritually. And He did. He replaced the torment of fear and panic with a peace that I wasn't able to find anywhere else.

I eventually left the Sheriff's Department and went to work as an Investigator at the Coroner's Office. My medical and law enforcement background were a perfect fit. The down side was that I lived, slept and breathed death. For almost two years I investigated death up close and personal. And eventually, it became too personal. After investigating nearly a thousand deaths, I was faced with a fatal auto accident involving a friend's wife. The death toll was enough. I changed jobs again and landed in the metropolitan police department where I continue to work today. But God's next lesson would serve to make my walk with Him even closer.

A domestic violence suspect had just shot at his family and responding officers. He then fled to an alley where my cover officer and I caught him. After a short standoff, the suspect fired his weapon at us and I returned fire, striking him twice. He later died of his injuries. It was a, "good shooting." Everyone was cleared. But as much death as I had seen, this was the first time that I had direct involvement in causing another person's death. The range of emotions was unexplainable. But what I can say is that God was there too. He was still in control. And that faith is what has made me even stronger.

My parting words are these; even now my faith continues to be challenged and life as a police officer has never been more difficult or dangerous. But I realized that in my mother's death, my brother's murder, and every time my own life has been in peril, God was always there. And through all of these tragic events, I have learned that if we will just seek God, we can find not only comfort in knowing that He loves us and cares for us but that we too can cross over from death and into eternal life.

"Joey"
Police officer

The Badge

You shall have no other gods before me. Exodus 20:3 (NIV)

To say that law enforcement is my "calling" is nothing short of an understatement. In fact, it would be safe to say that I've been a "cop" my entire life. I was always the biggest kid in school and I made bullies my personal project. Sticking up for others was something I took very seriously, literally patrolling the halls and playgrounds and making sure that weaker kids did not end up as fodder for those that would take advantage of them. Later in college, I knew that being a police officer was in my future and later graduated at the top of my police academy class. Once on the job, I flew through field training and it became readily apparent that I had been given a gift for police work.

While I had accepted Christ as my Savior in college, my personal life was certainly not what it should have been and the unique pressures and temptations present in our profession quickly consumed me. I lived and breathed police work, taking on every overtime assignment I could and coming home less and less. Eighty-hour weeks became the norm. My marriage suffered as a result and ultimately ended badly. As it turned out, I was married to "the badge" and little else mattered. Church and spending time in God's Word were things I simply didn't see the need for. Policing was my "ministry" and since I practically lived at work that was certainly more than enough. The badge had literally become my "god."

Beyond that, my personal life continued to stink. What time I did take away from the job was often spent in the gym or doing things with women that were certainly not godly. I didn't drink or carouse with the guys and my integrity at work was beyond question, but what was wrong with a little cussing and sex outside of marriage? I even justified it as being part of "the job." I failed to recognize my own pride, arrogance and self-righteous attitude about what I did for a living.

In 1995 I accepted a job in a mountain resort community and enthusiastically took on the alcohol and drug problems that tend to be endemic to such areas. My well intentioned zeal soon got me in trouble with a very liberal District Attorney who felt my arrests were upsetting the proverbial apple cart. I also allowed myself to take shortcuts (nothing illegal) in some of my reports that allowed me to spend less time in the station and more time on the street. Things came to a head when I arrested a local politician and close personal friend of the District Attorney for DUI. Apparently, she had a reputation for drunk driving but other officers had been "smart enough" to simply drive her home rather than arrest her. I was warned that by arresting her I was asking for trouble. But needless to say, I smugly ignored the warnings and booked her as I would any other. After all, I was too "righteous" and "ethical" to have done otherwise.

Feeling safe and proud for doing my job, I was shocked when the D.A. used one of my shortcuts to make a personal example out of me. To make a long story short, I found myself in every cop's worst nightmare. I was charged with two felonies and scared out of my wits. Feeling utterly alone, I reluctantly agreed to a plea bargain that would allow me to continue my career and the felonies were dropped. The judge suspended my sentence (a fine) and I was cleared to go back to work. However, it became immediately apparent that my reputation and credibility had been destroyed. I couldn't believe it. I had done nothing wrong and even saw my actions as "heroic." I also wondered, "How could a loving God allow one of his personally chosen "sheepdogs" to come to ruin, especially for having the courage to do the right thing?" To add salt to the wound, the arrest was never made public and the suspect went on to hold state office. I was angry at the system, angry at my profession, and yes, angry at God.

I ultimately resigned from the department with the idea that I would be quickly swept up by another agency. How wrong I was. I applied to more than forty different police agencies and while I tested at or near the top, I was always cut due to my background. I was miserable and became deeply depressed. I was forced to live off credit cards and barely kept my head above water with low paying security jobs. I began to have thoughts of suicide and would have likely gone through with it, had it not been for my Catholic upbringing that caused me to believe that by doing so would have condemned me to hell.

It took nearly two years to finally get back into law enforcement on a full-time basis but even then, I still failed to see it for the miracle that it was. My old habits quickly came back and while I earned a slew of awards and promotions, I continued to lack humility, live in sin, and keep God at a distance. My past continued to haunt me to the point that I literally left the country to take a position as a police supervisor on an overseas military installation. Utterly broken and crushed, I asked God to forgive me and recommitted my life to Christ.

Oh, what a loving and powerful God we serve! God had been waiting for just that moment to take the broken vessel and begin to rebuild it. He welcomed "His prodigal son" home and placed me in an elite unit with the State Police dealing with alcohol-related crimes. I became involved in a solid Bible-teaching church and with a great group of Christian officers who met weekly for Bible study and fellowship. But old habits die hard and I once again found myself overly immersed in work. I still managed to make it to church and Bible study but was often exhausted by the time I got there. My tough living also soon revealed some long-simmering health problems.

But again, God is faithful and refused to give up on me. As I grew and healed, I came to understand that God had a plan for me, as He does for each of us. And God continues to do miracles in my life. He brought me home and provided me with dual positions in law enforcement that force me to focus on things away from the job. Even more exciting and humbling was that God placed me in a position of ministry to, for, and about my fellow peace officers. In perhaps the biggest miracle of all, God also gave me a wonderful wife, ministry partner, and soul mate.

My past remains but I now see it as a means to keep me humble. I came to understand the meaning of the Commandment that says, "You shall have no other gods before me." Just as God loves us so much that He turned His back on His Son Jesus and allowed Him to die on a cross before raising Him up again, God took His protection from me just long enough to allow me to be broken in order to rebuild me into the man that He always intended me to be. While I still face problems, my confidence is now in Christ and I have a proper perspective when it comes to our special profession. I most certainly continue to protect the "sheep" from the "wolves," but I am now God's sheepdog with the primary goal of bringing glory to Him instead of myself. Most importantly, I am stoked about what God has in store for me both now and in the life to come.

"MC" Williams
Police Investigator

15

...AND NOTHING BUT THE TRUTH.

Unlikely allies

Rescue victims from their exploiters. Don't take advantage of the homeless, the orphans, the widows.
Jeremiah 22:3

In June of 2002, I saw a felony warrant for a man named Nelson Anderson in our daily bulletin. Later that day, I attempted to arrest him at his home. When I knocked on the front door, I was met by a slightly built, modestly dressed, yet beautiful woman named Veo. She acted suspicious and guarded and told me that Nelson wasn't home and that she didn't know when he'd be home. When I pressed, she told me that she had gone to California and when she returned, both Nelson and nearly everything they owned, was gone. Veo had no children and no other family. She was literally on her own, at eighty four years of age, and in failing health.

I returned the next day to check on her and thus began our unlikely friendship. As time passed, I discovered that Nelson had talked Veo into taking out a loan against her home so they'd have money to invest. She agreed and obtained a $101,000 loan. Then, while she was in California, Nelson cashed out the loan, cleaned out their bank account (including Veo's safe deposit box) and vanished.

But Veo was still responsible for the increasing loan payment and it eventually became more than her entire social security check. The only way for her to avoid foreclosure and be put out on the streets was to obtain a reverse mortgage. Unfortunately, that was easier said than done. Nelson's name was on the deed to the home and now he was gone.

I write this not to disparage Nelson, who has since died. Veo never spoke poorly of him, so I won't either. My aim in providing this background is so that you know how much Veo had to overcome in the last four years of her life. It seemed to be either a constant struggle for her financially or physically. But through it all, Veo remained a joyful, content, Godly woman.

With the help of a pro-bono lawyer, it was determined that in order for Veo to pay off the money that Nelson had taken, she would need to obtain a divorce and remove his name from the deed. She understood that this was the only way to avoid foreclosure, but she had to be repeatedly talked into going along with the divorce. Until the bitter end, she maintained hopeful that Nelson would call her to explain his actions, that she would gladly forgive him and that he would come home. I was in awe of her desire to forgive a man who left her in such dire straights with no explanation. Eventually, the divorce was final and we got her finances straightened out as much as possible. But Veo was never happy about it. Even when she found out that Nelson had died, she wondered aloud if she should fly out of state and help in covering his funeral costs.

Shortly after we first met, Veo became part of the Andrew's family. She spent most holidays and special occasions with us and was always a welcome addition in our home. She also loved my son, Ian as if he were her own. They had a special relationship that was never more evident than when he visited her in the hospital during the final six weeks of her life. I told her many times that she was a blessing to my family and I pray that she knew I meant it.

Thanks to Veo, I've had the chance to see pure calm in the face of a storm, enduring faithfulness and reliance on God, and a pervasive joy and contentment that can't be diminished. Veo is one of the people who was surely welcomed to her eternal home with the words, "Well done, good and faithful servant."

I thank God that I saw the warrant for Nelson in the bulletin. If I'd missed it, I would have missed an incredible experience. My family and I were honored to have an opportunity to come to the aid of a helpless widow and to care for one of "the least of these." It's often said that those who serve end up feeling more blessed than those who are being served, and that was certainly true in this case. In serving Veo, we saw true gratitude, a beautiful, unshakable faith, an ever present willingness to forgive and an exemplary love for God. It also gave my young son an opportunity to both give and receive the kind of love that God wants us to give... a love without regard to race, money, education or anything else that might stand in the way.

God used a young, white, upper-middle class cop, to love and care for an elderly, black, poverty-stricken widow. And through our obedience to His word, my life and the lives of my family members were changed forever.

Daniel Andrews
Corporal

The faith of a centurion

The greatest faith is not the one that never wavers; it is the one that reaches up for help when it does. -Anonymous

I entered policing in the turbulent 60's. American society was in turmoil. Anti-government, anti-war and anti-authority sentiments were the order of the day. Upon graduation from the academy I was sent to the most disorderly, violent district in the city. Within my first twenty minutes on the street I had a rude awakening: not everyone liked the police or what they represented in my world, as much as I did. In my world, I love and admired the police. They were trustworthy and courageous. My dad was a career police officer. Many of his friends were police officers and my earliest memories are of being surrounded by blue uniforms. But even growing up within the police culture, I was astounded and shocked at how much I didn't know about police-community relationships.

In my first week, I was spit at, threatened, assaulted and found myself fighting for my life with three homicide suspects. What shook me to my core however was how much hatred was directed at me because of my color…blue. I had been raised in a Catholic family and attended Catholic schools all the way through college. Those Jesuit priests, whom I am forever grateful to, imbued me with a strong motivation for service and a profound desire to serve God by serving others. But despite my honorable motives to be of service and to help remedy the ills of society as best I could, I was stereotyped as a, "pig" and "oppressor" by many of those I was risking my life to protect.

But while I must admit that I still loved the job despite those things (I even hated the idea of taking days off for fear of missing something), it was also changing me inside. I was becoming hard, cynical and suspicious. As I witnessed the ability of people to inflict senseless violence on each other and the abuse and neglect they subjected their children to, I asked, "How could a good and loving God allow this to happen?" This was especially the case when the victims were elderly, young or otherwise innocent individuals who were just trying to live a peaceful existence. I am ashamed to admit that I began to question my deeply ingrained faith.

The downward spiral of my faith was exacerbated by the loss of police friends who were severely injured, killed in the line of duty or who had taken their own lives. In the olden days, we lost two to three good officers each year to suicide; a trend that has thankfully relented but one that unfortunately still occurs far too often. Also contributing to the downward slide of my faith were changes that were occurring within the Catholic Church. All these factors converged to make me what I had always feared becoming, a fallen away Catholic.

And while I did retain my pure service intentions and became more committed than ever to protecting the, "sheep from the wolves," I became known as a hard working, dedicated officer who was also a "thumper." At the first indication of resistance, things were settled quickly and decisively. I was involved in several shootings, including one in which myself and several brother officers were fired at six times at point blank range and yet remarkably were not hit. It began to occur to me that God was watching over me and I pined over my estrangement from both Him and the Church.

To make a long story made short, I reengaged with both my faith and the Church and felt an immeasurable relief. I also began to mature on the job and realized that talk often works as well, or better than, force. And as I began to promote through the ranks, I quickly realized the obvious; the best cops are those with the courage of a lion and an even bigger heart. Those are the treasured cops who can seek out and arrest the predators while maintaining a personal purity of intention and motivation. Those are the ones who can be the terror of criminals but a strong shoulder for the victims, children and society's lost souls to lean on. And it is obvious that they are the ones who have an anchor in their lives that allows them to possess such highly developed coping mechanisms. The best of which is a strong faith in God and a commitment to live out their faith.

I can unequivocally testify to the fact that police work without God is to miss an opportunity to live the mission that Jesus gave to us: feed my sheep, defend the defenseless and to give far more than you will ever receive in return.

Mike

Police Officer/Trainer

A regular Joe

May I never boast except in the cross of our Lord Jesus Christ. Galatians 6:14 (NIV)

I grew up in a Christian household and remember feeling God's presence in my life even as a kid. But I eventually stopped going to church, fell out of the Christian scene and began to party hard. That is, until that lifestyle didn't provide the peace that I thought it would. I eventually came back to Christ at the end of High School and went from being popular to being a Jesus freak. But that was cool; I had found the true peace that only comes through Jesus Christ.

I'd always wanted to be a cop, ever since watching CHiP's as a kid in the late 70's. But I'm not your super-cop with ripped biceps and a SWAT logo on my lapel. I'm just a regular Joe, average in size and looks. In fact, the cops who still party hard would probably consider me a nerd. So when I take care of things that usually only the tactical guys handle, I have to give credit to God.

One morning, I got in my car and headed out to my beat after briefing. After stopping by the local Starbucks, I started driving down the road when dispatch aired a BOLO for a hit-and-run vehicle. The vehicle was unique and described as an older model, blue, Ford pickup with a, "For sale" sign in the window. I thought, "I can't miss that." A few moments later, I saw a truck matching that description and watched as a shady looking character with long hair and a flannel shirt, parked at a local motel and jumped out.

If you've ever read the Calibre Press books, this guy fulfilled the, "No look rule." He glanced at me but immediately looked away and walked quickly into the motel. My adrenaline raised a little as I knew this guy was up to something more than just a hit-and-run. I called out my location at the motel and walked to the front desk. The desk person told me that he saw the male walk in but that he wasn't a customer. I did a "quick-peek" down the hallway and saw the guy give a "quick-peek" back at me! I called for a cover car and told the guy to walk towards me.

As he began to walk towards me, I asked him for ID. Of course, he said he didn't have any. I went to grab his arm to search him and asked him if he had any weapons. As soon as I said, "weapons" he took off running out the door. What happened next was unique for me, as I responded differently than how I had been trained. I simultaneously grabbed my radio with my left hand and my gun with my right. I called out that I was in a foot chase and started to sprint after him. I heard other officers call out that they were enroute emergent and I could hear the sirens in the background. As I came around the corner of the building, the male had stopped and was facing me. At gunpoint, I gave him verbal commands to put his hands up and lay face down on the ground. He responded by saying that he had a gun. I told him that if I saw it pointed at me, he would be dead. I saw in his eyes and demeanor that he didn't think I was going to react the way I did. After my help arrived, I was able to hook the guy up. Under his flannel shirt, he had a loaded Glock in a shoulder holster and two extra magazines. When I later searched his truck, I found another gun, burglary tools and a map of the construction sites where the hit-and-run had occurred.

After reflecting on it, I saw how God intervened and got me through this scenario. I believe the guy ran around the corner and was going to shoot it out with me, only he saw the barrel of my gun and decided I had the upper hand. Whether my tactics were good or bad, I was told never (unless being actively shot at) to have your gun out during a foot chase, as you can clench your hand and accidentally pull the trigger. Yet, I had done exactly the opposite, even when I hadn't seen a weapon. I praised God out loud in front of the other people who were with me on that call. He had prompted me to do what I did.

I've since changed jobs and now work for a larger department. Most of the guys on my shift are either believers or have a Christian background. Coincidence? No, that's God! Just the other day I was having a bad start. Although I got my Starbucks Iced Americano, I had some things on my mind. So I prayed and asked God to give me a dope arrest, as that always cheers me up. Two minutes later, a nice Audi blew a stop sign. The driver had a cancelled license, a warrant and yes, a bunch of dope, a grand in cash, and some scales and baggies. Possession with Intent to Distribute. It's a good day again.

Although I'm a cop and I try hard to do what is right every day, I still fail miserably. Maybe not in the world's eyes, but in a Biblical sense. I'm a sinner. Most cops hate to say they're bad in any way, but according to the Bible, we're all sinners (which simply means that we've "missed the mark") and I've missed the mark with God every day of my life. Maybe I didn't sin by killing, robbing or stealing like you find in the statute books, but I didn't measure up to the sinless life that God requires. But thankfully, Jesus Christ took my sins, died to pay for them and later rose from the dead to defeat them, forever. And believing that is what makes me (and you) forgiven.

"Josh"
Police Officer

16

THE COLD, HARD FACTS

Evidence: *That which is legally submitted...as a means of ascertaining the truth.*

B ut what if no one saw the professor murder Mr. Body in the conservatory with the candlestick? Can we know, beyond a reasonable doubt, that he indeed committed the crime in question? Absolutely. Remember, there is no such thing as a perfect crime.

As investigators examined Mr. Body's corpse, they were able to determine that the time of death was 8:05 p.m. They then checked Mr. Body's video surveillance system. They found that good professor was the only one, besides Mr. Body, to enter the conservatory all evening. The video revealed that he entered the conservatory at 7:53 p.m. and later exited at 8:12 p.m. Just before and shortly after the murder.

Due to the strange, arc shaped wound on Mr. Body's head, some clever thinking and thorough searching, the investigators were able to locate the murder weapon on the dining room table. It contained both the professor's finger-prints and a blood sample that matched Mr. Body's. They were then able to find hair follicles and clothing fibers under Mr. Body's fingernails due to the struggle with his assailant. Both samples matched the professor's DNA. And finally, they recovered a shoe print on the conservatory floor. It matched the professor's shoe size, style and imprint.

When investigator's arrested the professor, he agreed to talk. Believing that he was able to slip inside the conservatory unnoticed, murder Mr. Body, slip out unnoticed and replace the candlestick to the dining room table, he thought he didn't have anything to worry about. The professor waived his Miranda Rights and stated, "After dinner, I spent the remainder of the evening in the study before retiring to bed at around 10:15 p.m." The problem with providing that statement was the video that would eventually prove him to be a liar.

Now, a defense attorney would present to a jury that any combination of those facts was mere, "circumstantial evidence." They would argue that just because some of those things are true, it doesn't mean that their client is guilty. Sound familiar? But what happens when all the facts are true? The professor's defense attorney must suddenly become a "good" defense attorney [if there is such a term] and urge his client to accept a plea bargain as a means of avoiding death row.

So with that in mind, here are the cold, hard facts that support the book's premise of becoming spiritually bulletproof. You be the jury and decide if the evidentiary facts listed below are true or not, because really, the final verdict is up to you.

Exhibit A: Your own confession

You don't need a Bible to tell you that you sin. You already know that. Now, you may not want to look at yourself as a sinner but if we're going to examine all the evidence, you have to admit, you're a sinner. Come on, admit it. The

Bible says, "If we claim that we've never sinned, we out and out contradict God- make a liar out of him." (1 John 1:8-10). So stop fooling yourself. Hesitant? That's okay, let's go through it. We'll start out light. Ever break the law? Any law? What about speeding down the highway? Failing to signal? Cruising through a stop sign?

"Aw, come on, those aren't sins."

What about the Ten Commandments then? Ever told a lie?

"Ah, yeah, one or two."

What does that make you?

"A sinner?"

No, specifically. What does that make you?

"I'm not a liar."

How many times then do you have to lie to make you a liar? Isn't it true, that if you tell one lie, it makes you a liar?

"Yeah, I guess you're right."

Have you ever stolen anything?

"No."

"Aw, Come on, you just admitted that you're a liar."

Ever stolen something, even if it was small?

"Yeah."

And what does that make you?

"A thief?"

Exactly.

And Jesus said that if you look at a woman and lust after her, you commit adultery with her in your heart. Ever done that?

Long pause...

"Yeah, plenty of times."

There you go. Proof from your own admission, that you're a lying, thieving adulterer at heart. And someday you'll have to face God for that. And we've only looked at three of the Ten Commandments!

So if you were to stand in front of God right now, would you be innocent or guilty?

"Guilty."

Now you're getting what the Bible says is true, "We all start out as sinners...There's nobody living right, not even one...They've all taken the wrong turn" (Romans 3:9-20).

Exhibit B: The judge's gavel

But you don't have to be a liar, thief or adulterer to be separated from God. One sin, one mistake, one selfish, prideful moment and we are in need of becoming right again. But remember that it's not so much *the* sin, as what the sin *did* to us? That's really what we need the Bible to illuminate for us, the penalty part of it all.

Because if I were to then ask you, "So do you think you'll go to heaven or hell?" The typical response is, "Heaven." And if that's your response, why did you respond that way? Is it because you think God is good and he'll overlook your "small" sins?

"Yeah, God is a good God. He wouldn't send me to hell for little stuff like that."

Does a good judge punish a good man if the good man committed a crime? Of course. Even if the crime was only a traffic infraction? Yes. The judge says, "Because I'm good, I have to see that you're punished."

Justice requires punishment. Period.

Being *good* isn't part of the equation. That's our own messed up idea. Nobody goes to heaven by being good enough. God says that we go to heaven, "by grace...through faith" (Ephesians 2:8-9, NIV). It's not about being good. And for that you should be glad. How would you ever know if you were good *enough*? Sure, you'd probably be better than a murderer. But are you as good as Mother Theresa? You're definitely not as good as Mother Theresa. So what's the standard? And according to whom? Every religion is different. Who's right?

According to the Bible, nobody's good enough. It says, "The wages of sin is death" (Romans 6:23, NIV). Period. It doesn't matter if you're a good person. You're a sinner and your sin deserves death. It's like having a cancer inside of you. Without the cure, it's going to kill you. The Bible says, "Your wound [sin] is incurable, your injury beyond healing" (Jeremiah 30:12-13, NIV).

So if you only understand one thing about sin, understand this; it's not a slap on the wrist. It's a wound that we cannot cure, an injury we cannot heal and its final payment, is death.[6]

Exhibit C: Lights and that obnoxious siren

And if that's where we were left, we'd be in a pretty miserable situation. But that's where Christianity sets itself apart. It's not up to us. Nor is God that cruel to leave us wondering if we made the grade. He tells us up front that we're all sinners, that we don't make the cut regardless of how good we think we are, and that the only way to ever be pardoned from that death sentence is to pull over and stop for the lights and siren behind us.

That's the amazing thing about Christianity. It's not just another religion. It's a relationship between God and the man he created. And he is pursuing us to regain that right relationship that he intended. The Bible says it in an awesome way, "We throw open our doors for God and discover at the same moment that he has already thrown open his door to us" (Romans 5:1-2).

As much as I disdain fireman,* it would be like if you accidentally set your house ablaze and before your fingers could frantically dial 911, that obnoxiously loud fire truck was already parked in front of your house to save the day! That's how much God wants to save you. The moment you choose to be rescued, he's already there, just waiting to do it.

Exhibit D: Not for sale

In addition to the incredible truth that God pursues us, is the fact that when we stop to see what he's got to offer, it's free. God's not running some scam like some ambulance chasing lawyer. The Bible says, "This is how much God loved the world: He gave his Son" so that, "by *believing* in him, *anyone* can have a whole and lasting life" (John 3:16).

Did you get the "free" part in that? All you have to do is *believe* that what he says is true. Nothing down, no interest, not for sale. 100% totally free. And it's so important to God that you get that, he emphasizes again. It's an offer to *anyone*. It's not an offer that only the rich can afford or the powerful can attain. It's available to anyone willing to believe, including you, no matter what you've ever done. And that even goes for those of you still hesitant to admit that you're a lying, thieving adulterer.

Exhibit E: The Cross

As great as it is that God pursues us and that what he has to offer us is free, the penalty for our sin still had to be paid for. Our problem had yet to be resolved. And because of our sin, we were incapable of paying our own ticket even if we wanted to. No, in order to satisfy the payment, God required a *perfect sacrifice* for our sins. And since we aren't perfect, we needed a perfect person to step in the way and pay it for us. And that meant an innocent, perfect person had to die in our place. And that's exactly what Jesus Christ did for you. The perfect man, one that no one could find any fault in, was put to death on a cross so that, "Your covenant with death will be annulled" (Isaiah 28:18, NIV). Jesus Christ was the only one that could ever make us bulletproof. He was the only one that could ever fix the cancer inside of us. He was the only one that could take a death sentence and turn it into life.

I love the way *The Message* says it, "Think of it! All sins forgiven, the slate wiped clean, that old arrest warrant canceled and nailed to Christ's cross" (Colossians 2:14-15). I can't tell you how elated [the few] people have been when I've arrested them, only to find out that their arrest warrant had been canceled. Their slate is wiped clean and there is nothing left hanging over them. The cuffs come off and they're no longer in bondage. They're free.

But even more earth shattering is that God didn't wait until we started doing things right to take care of it. That cancer inside us was never going to get any better. The Bible says that, "God demonstrates his own love for us in this: *while we were still sinners*, Christ died for us" (Romans 5:8, NIV). That's the biggest proof of all. We can understand someone dying for a person worth dying for, right? Cops, soldiers, firefighters and everyday heroes do it all the time. They willingly die for each other and those they serve. But have we ever heard of someone showing up at a complete stranger's criminal execution and willingly take their place? Never! Who would die for someone else, when that person was so worthy to die for the heinous crimes they committed? Only Jesus.

Exhibit F: An empty grave

But none of that really means anything at all.

"What?!"

None of that means anything at all, if God had not raised Jesus Christ from the dead. And Jesus was raised back to life. The Bible says, "They took him down from the cross and buried him. And then God raised him from death. There is no disputing that. He appeared over and over again many times and places to those who had know him well in the Galilean years, and these same people continue to give witness that he is alive" (Acts 13:29-31).

That's the whole significance of Easter. Yes, Jesus died on a cross to pay for our sins, but the fact that God raised him from death is what gave him power over death. Without the resurrection, his death would have been meaningless. Death would have defeated him. Death would have won. But the truth is that it didn't win. Jesus Christ lived and breathed and walked the earth before ascending back into heaven. And because of that, the Bible says, "Death has been swallowed up in victory. Where, O death, is your victory? Where, O death, is your sting?" (1 Corinthians 15:54-55, NIV).

"That's what baptism into the life of Jesus means. When we are lowered into the water, it is like the burial of Jesus; when we are raised up out of the water, it is like the resurrection of Jesus. Could it be any clearer? Our old way of life was nailed to the Cross with Christ. If we get included in Christ's sin conquering death, we also get include in his life saving resurrection. *Never again will death have the last word*" (Romans 6:3-11).

Exhibit G: A voided ticket

God has a ticket in his hand. It has someone's name on it. Maybe a lying, thieving, adulterer's name. It says the penalty for their sins, regardless how big or small they are, is death. But he's also holding a Void Stamp. And whoever is willing to let Jesus Christ pay the penalty for their sin, he's willing to void their ticket.

Pardoned.

Aquitted.

Free.

Those people become perfect as they stand before him. Not because of anything they did. But because of what Jesus did for them. That may not even sound believable. It may sound too good to be true. But the Bible makes it very clear:

"God sent me [Jesus] to announce *pardon* to the prisoners" (Luke 4:16-21).

"Anyone who trusts in him [Jesus] is *acquitted*" (John 3:18).

"Because of the sacrifice of the Messiah [Jesus]...*we're free* people- free of penalty and punishments chalked up by all our misdeeds" (Ephesians 1:7).

And if we're free and clear of all charges against us, everything between God and us is cool. We're in right standing with him. "Everyone who believes in this raised up Jesus is *declared good and right and whole before God*" (Acts 13:39). God actually changes us from death row criminal to friend. Check it out. "Become friends with God. How you say? In Christ. God put the wrong on him who never did anything wrong, so we could be put right with God" (2 Corinthians 5:21).

And if God did all of that for us when we were in *that* condition, can you imagine what he'll do for us when everything is right with him? Well, there's no reason to imagine because here's the two most important promises that God makes for those of us on his side: the first promise is that we don't have to face life alone any longer. God himself says, "I'll never let you down, never walk off and leave you" (Hebrews 13:5). And in the infamous 23rd Psalm, David acknowledges that promise by saying, "Even though I walk through the valley of the shadow of death, I will fear no evil, *for you are with me*" (Psalm 23:4, NIV). So when you choose to live life God's way, be assured, that no matter what life throws at you or what valley you find yourself in, God will never let you down. He'll be there with you, even in the thick of it.

The second promise is that we'll spend eternity in heaven. Jesus said, "I am going there [heaven] to prepare a place for you…that you also may be where I am" (John 14:2-3, NIV). And this guy Paul, who God entrusted to write much of the New Testament, wrote, "But now that you have been set free from sin…*the result is eternal life*" (Romans 6:22, NIV). No matter what we ever face in life, without taking away the real life pain of it, the end result is that we conquer it all through Jesus Christ. We conquer it, not necessarily in the physical but in the spiritual, not necessarily in the temporal but in the eternal. And we conquer it, not because of our own ability, resources or talent, (by no means!) but because Christ has made everything cool with God on our behalf.

Exhibit H: Free will

You don't have to slow down, pull over or do anything else that you don't want to do. And that's the way God intended it. He may not want you to drive off in the wrong direction, knowing that you're on your way down a dead end road with no guardrail, but if that's the life you choose, he isn't stopping you from doing it. It's called, free will. And the reason he gave it to you is the same reason he must punish the wrong, he's good. Only an evil god would force you to do what you didn't want to do.

A guy named Joshua said it this way, "If you decide that it's a bad thing to worship God, then choose a god you'd rather serve…" (Joshua 24:15).

No one's twisting your arm. If what God is offering you isn't for you, choose someone or something else. Because make no doubt about it, you serve someone or something, even if that someone is you. And if you make that choice, God just has one question for you, "How's that working out for you?" And if or when your answer to God's question is, "Not so good" just glance in that rearview mirror again. He didn't go anywhere. He's still there. Following, waiting and hoping to give you the best life you could ever have.

The final verdict

So I don't know where you ended up with all of this but I'd just like to leave you with this…if you believe that what God has for you is better than what you've got going for yourself, you can have it right now. Just be real with yourself, your mistakes, and your need for Jesus Christ and let him make things right between you and God once and for all.

> *"Say the welcoming word- Jesus is my Master…*
> *That's it.*
> *You're not doing anything; you're simply calling*
> *out to God, trusting him to do it for you.*
> *That's salvation.*
> *With your whole being you embrace God setting*
> *things right, and then you say it, right out loud:*
> *God has set everything right between him and*
> *me!"* Romans 10:4-10

That's not a guarantee that life won't slam into you. It's not a guarantee that you won't face pain, illness, suffering, financial difficulty, broken relationships or even death. And it's not a guarantee that life will be easy. It's a promise that the God of the universe will be with you when life is hard and more importantly, that you will be with him when all of that no longer matters. That's the bulletproof guarantee. It's more spiritual than physical and more eternal than temporal. And for me, that's the greatest assurance of all.

---

* I say that jokingly. I have a wonderful respect for "hose draggers" and their "work." But I really do hate lawyers.

A FINAL WORD

As a word of encouragement towards your new found life, I leave you with this one last bulletproof analogy:

While bulletproof vests have come a long way technologically, they are not designed for comfort. They are simply designed to do what the human body is incapable of doing for itself; to stop incoming bullets from penetrating the body's outer shell and destroying its internal vital organs.

That being the case, ballistic armor manufactures suggest that body armor be replaced every five years for maximum effectiveness. So every five years, I am issued a new bulletproof vest. And every five years, I am uncomfortable all over again. When I put that new, stiff bulletproof vest on, there is a certain break-in period until my body and vest begin to conform to each other. For weeks, I tug, pull, adjust and otherwise struggle with it. And while body armor never becomes totally comfortable, eventually that vest becomes a more natural part of me.

It's the same way with God. God never said that accepting his bulletproof offer is going to be comfortable. In fact, Jesus warns us upfront that choosing what he has to offer is going to cause some discomfort and disruption in our lives. Jesus didn't pay our ticket and make us right with God to fulfill our American dream and to save our decaying, dying physical body. He did what we were incapable of doing; to stop the bullets of sin from destroying our eternal, *spiritual* body. Don't let that burst your bubble. That's a good thing.

As God wraps himself around you from the inside out, there is a tendency to tug, pull, make adjustments and struggle against this new bulletproof fabric that he's weaving through our lives. And that's okay. Its proof that he's now a part of your life and that you're getting used to living life a new way. A different way. A better way. Eventually, your relationship with God will become a more natural part of who you are as you grow in the grace of God.

I can't promise you that being bulletproof is going to be comfortable. But what I can promise you is that the protection God offers far outweighs ever living life without it.

NOTES

1. Johnny Cash reference: *The Man in Black* (Grand Rapids, MI: Zondervan Publishing House 1975). Pg.61.
2. State Statute 18-18-405. Colorado Peace Officer's Statutory Source Book 1996/1997 Edition Pg. 1-7 thru 8, Pg. 9-12.
3. Awareness Spectrum, from the author's police academy training lectures. 1997.
4. Basic police tactics from the author's police academy training lectures. 1997.
5. Brennan Manning reference: The Ragamuffin Gospel (Sisters, OR: Multnomah Publishers, Inc. 1990) Pg. 31-32.
6. Exhibit A, B: Ray Comfort, *Hell's Best Kept Secret,* http://www.livingwaters.com/helps/HellsBestKeptSecret.pdf (visited February 1, 2008). Hell's Best Kept Secret is non-copyrighted and duplication is encouraged.

All quotes taken from www.brainyquote.com with the following exceptions: James Rogers (www.quotationspage.com); Shakespeare (Chapter 13), (www.william-shake-speare.info/shakespeare-play-king-henry-vi-part-2.htm); Sun Tzu (Chapter 8), *The Art of War,* (Filiquarian Publishing, LLC, 2006). Pg. 44; Sun Tzu (Chapter 11), *The Art of War,* (Filiquarian Publishing, LLC, 2006). Pg. 7; Sun Tzu (Chapter

12), *The Art of War,* (Filiquarian Publishing, LLC, 2006). Pg. 32; and Anonymous quotes, which are the authors.

ACKNOWLEDGEMENTS

Writing this book has taken far more time, effort and frustration than I ever thought possible. Much of it was like a typical male driving experience: I knew where I wanted to go, kept getting lost along the way and was less than enthusiastic about stopping and asking for directions. Thankfully, many people noticed the obviously lost look on my face and were kind enough to not only turn my map right-side-up, but to point me in the right direction time and time again. Without them, I would have surely hit "Delete" and ended the misery of driving around in so many literary circles. I can not thank each of you enough, but in a humble attempt, I must at least try.

God. First of all, thank you for pursuing me, allowing Jesus to pay my ticket and for making everything between us cool. For that, I am eternally thankful, literally. Thank you for giving your message to me in such a tangible way that I couldn't help but understand it better, grasp it fuller and have the desire to share it with others. Thank you for that privilege and honor. Why you would entrust men so unworthy as me, to share your redemptive, rescuing plan is mind blowing. I only pray that I presented it in a manner worthy of the gospel. And last but not least, thank you for continuing to provide me with your endless love and grace each and every day, for without it, I would certainly be lost.

T. You are the most beautiful person I've ever met. Thank you for being my biggest fan. Your endless patience, sacrifice and tireless support are what made this book possible. I can think of no higher praise to say than for any souls affected by its message, they have only you and God to thank as they enter into wondrous life.

Bob, for everything you have contributed to my life. You have made me a better cop, a better poker player and a better man. Thanks for being such a great partner and friend, for fearlessly fighting by my side on so many occasions and for your time and effort in editing a haystack full of needles.

I want to thank those responsible for making this book a reality; Ron Mazellan for your vision and insight and for planting the seed several years ago; Les Stobbe for seeing what others could not see and for all of your guidance; Lynn of Genesis Publishing Group for providing me with *Hell's Best Kept Secret*; Jim, Mike, Tim and Gino who took the time to read through a messy, flawed manuscript and endorsed it anyways. I am humbled by your support. And with much appreciation, Dave Grossman, who has been one of the most generous, humble men I have ever met. It has been an honor to have you a part of this project. But mostly, I want to thank my pastor and friend, Jim Burgen. You've reintroduced me to God in so many fresh and amazing ways and for that I am eternally grateful. Thanks for teaching me, "a better way to live life," the "Me Too" concept and for your time, direction and mentoring in this project; all of which I hold as invaluable.

I would also like to thank those within my warrior circle; to all my boys in the Bureau of Prisons, but especially Big Pipes. Thanks for making my life in the joint tolerable. To my Chief of Police, Kathy B. and Rick for supporting me in both my achievements and my failures. You have made this journey possible; to all of my police instructors, teammates and cops who I have had the privilege to work with over the past ten years. You have taught me, trained me, and watched my back and for that, I thank you; a special thanks to "Pete," Bish, Tommy and Troy for your willingness to be a part of this; to "Cool Hand" Luke for forgiving me every time that I have failed at acting like a Christian, which was often; and to Mike O'Neill for all of your support and encouragement. I would follow you into any battle, even to the gates of hell.

To the cops who contributed your testimony to the project, I thank you. Your faith to step out of the boat and into unknown waters was inspiring. And while it was a privilege and honor to read your stories, it is an even greater privilege and honor for you to allow me to share them with others.

I want to thank all of my family and friends who supported me in this crazy endeavor but especially; Vada Jane, who I love most dearly. You believed in me when I didn't believe in myself. Thanks for standing in the gap. To my posse, Jeff, Floyd and Dallas (and Lisa too) whose affect on my life has been substantial. And to my girl, Phyl for your continued support, which often meant the difference between quitting and not and for no other reason but just because you are you.

I want to give a very special thanks to the guy who wanted to kill me in a dark and filthy alley. You validated my literary resume, of which I would not have had the qualification, or the understanding, to write about the truths of what being bulletproof is all about. Thank you for being a significant piece of God's beautiful puzzle in my life. I continue to pray that you will find his amazing grace.

Finally, I want to thank the lyrical influence that made a difference in the direction this project went: Motley Crue, N.E.R.D., Sammy Hagar, Disciple, the Newsboys, United, Third Day, Jeremy Camp, Johnny Cash, The Beastie Boys, Day of Fire, John Newton (the author of Amazing Grace) and David Crowder who has given me new meaning to the words "Nunzilla" and worship.

Printed in the United States
132812LV00005B/1/P